Unde ~~rstanding 4-5-Year~~ **-Olds**

Understanding Your Child Series

The Tavistock Clinic has an international reputation as a centre of excellence for training, clinical mental health work, research and scholarship. Written by professionals working in the Child and Family and the Adolescent Departments, the guides in this series present balanced and sensitive advice that will help adults to become, or to feel that they are, "good enough" parents. Each book concentrates on a key transition in a child's life from birth to adolescence, looking especially at how parents' emotions and experiences interact with those of their children. The titles in the Understanding Your Child series are essential reading for new and experienced parents, relatives, friends and carers, as well as for the multi-agency professionals who are working to support children and their families.

other titles in the series

Understanding
4–5-Year-Olds

Lesley Maroni

Jessica Kingsley Publishers
London and Philadelphia

First published in 2007
by Jessica Kingsley Publishers
116 Pentonville Road
London N1 9JB, UK
and
400 Market Street, Suite 400
Philadelphia, PA 19106, USA

www.jkp.com

Library of Congress Cataloging in Publication Data
A CIP catalog record for this book is available from the Library of Congress

British Library Cataloguing in Publication Data
A CIP catalogue record for this book is available from the British Library

ISBN 978 1 84310 534 3

Printed and bound in Great Britain by
Athenaeum Press, Gateshead, Tyne and Wear

Contents

Acknowledgements

With grateful thanks to Jane Purchase and all the children in her reception class both past – my own two sons – and present. Also to my husband, Harry, for his patient reading of the text and his thoughtful suggestions, and to my colleagues and parents for their generous sharing of material with me.

Foreword

The Tavistock Clinic has an international reputation as a centre of excellence for training, clinical mental health work, research and scholarship. Established in 1920, its history is one of groundbreaking work. The original aim of the Clinic was to offer treatment which could be used as the basis of research into the social prevention and treatment of mental health problems, and to teach these emerging skills to other professionals. Later work turned towards the treatment of trauma, the understanding of conscious and unconscious processes in groups, as well as important and influential work in developmental psychology. Work in perinatal bereavement led to a new understanding within the medical profession of the experience of stillbirth, and of the development of new forms of support for mourning parents and families. The development in the 1950s and 1960s of a systemic model of psychotherapy, focusing on the interaction between children and parents and within families, has grown into the substantial body of theoretical knowledge and therapeutic techniques used in the Tavistock's training and research in family therapy.

The Understanding Your Child series has an important place in the history of the Tavistock Clinic. It has been issued in a completely new form three times: in the 1960s, the 1990s, and in 2004. Each time the authors, drawing on their clinical background and specialist training, have set out to reflect on the extraordinary story of "ordinary development" as it was observed and experienced at the time. Society changes, of course, and so has this series, as it attempts to make sense of everyday accounts of the ways in which a developing child interacts with his or her parents, carers and the wider world. But within this changing scene there has been something constant, and it is best described as a continuing enthusiasm for a view of development which recognizes the importance of the strong feelings and emotions experienced at each stage of development.

So far in the series, a volume has been devoted to each year. This is the first book to bring together two years of development, and to consider them as a complex whole.

In focusing on 4–5-year-olds, this book documents the changes that take place when children start to explore relationships beyond the family, and the world of friendships. Children at this age are also intensely curious about the world around them, which can prove to be both a source of joy and exhaustion. Lesley Maroni offers a vivid description of children at this important stage of development, and offers approachable insights for parents and the professionals who work with them.

Jonathan Bradley
Child Psychotherapist
General Editor of the Understanding Your Child series

Introduction

The aim of this short book is to try to imagine the lives of four- to five-year-olds from their perspective as they gradually move away from a passionate attachment to their families and turn towards the wider world of school and life outside the family.

The primary focus of children at this age is on relationships, especially adult relationships. In other words, how do people join up? How did Mummy and Daddy join up? Where do I fit in this? In order to be able to form friendships of her own (I will use "she" and "he" in alternate chapters when referring to children of either gender), the four- to five-year-old has to have moved from the wish to have an exclusive relationship with one parent, in order to make a space for the other parent as part of what now becomes a triangular relationship. It is in this way that a child develops a sense of herself as different from but connected to the parental couple. When in reality there is only one parent, the child simply works harder to incorporate the idea of a third, and will ask numerous questions about the absent parent to try to puzzle things out.

A single mother or a single father can, of course, have the qualities of the other, i.e. a mother can find a firmer, more authoritative voice within her just as a father can show a softer side when necessary. The family consisting of mother and father and children is frequently disrupted nowadays by separation and divorce. There may well be new families formed with a stepparent who brings his or her own children into the mix. New babies can be born, to add half-siblings to what becomes an extended and confusing family system. To take all these different permutations into account would make this into another kind of book entirely, and so I will be using a two-parent family as a model, partly because children themselves have this model in their minds, however different their reality is.

In some ways this age is a precursor of what is to come during the adolescent years, in terms of the struggle to balance the continuing need for parental care and attention with the desire for independence. The four- to five-year-old begins to look outwards as she forms relationships with her peers but she also wants to be able to go back to her mother for reassurance.

One of the most delightful aspects of children in this age group is their endless curiosity about the world and their wish to understand their place in it. This is the time of questions: Where do I come from? Why...? How...? etc., sometimes to the extent of driving parents mad (and testing their own knowledge of the world). "But *why* is the sky blue?" one four-year-old asked repeatedly over the course of a few months. His mother, after many thoughtful answers, ended up saying in exasperation, "Just because it is, that's why!" He then went on to ask other similar questions, mostly unanswerable, such as "Where is God?"

The child is also beginning to be able to empathize, in other words, to put herself into others' shoes and imagine how they might be feeling. This ability to feel concern for others and care about their feelings is a major milestone in her development. A little girl on hearing that the younger brother of a friend of hers had accidentally locked himself in the bathroom, said, "He must have been really scared that his daddy wouldn't be able to open the door." However, when it comes to siblings, being able to "read" them goes with knowing exactly how to wind them up and what will annoy them the most!

This, of course, is also the age at which the first major transition takes place – when, before, going to nursery school or playgroup was a choice, now going to school becomes a legal requirement. Learning is more formalized, although in most reception classes nowadays there is a good balance between "work" and play. Some children manage their anxiety by being intellectually able when they are not so socially at ease. Other lucky ones flourish in all ways. But most come somewhere in between, sometimes feeling left out and rejected and sometimes being right at the centre of things. Children have to learn to share a teacher's attention; they also learn that they are not the special and only one.

Friendships are becoming more stable, and more based on shared experience. When the rising five-year-old starts proper school, even if this is simply a transition from the nursery part of the school to the reception class, it helps enormously if she has firm friends who will be going on this journey with her.

It is important to feel known and accepted by others outside the family. You can often see the delight on a child's face when she locates a friend in the playground, and the despair when the friend is absent.

But all children of this age have one thing in common – a desire to find out about their expanding world.

1

Family Life

Life at home

"Look what I can do!"

It is easy to be taken by surprise by the four- to five-year-old's swings between the desire to show off his new-found skills and his burgeoning independence, and a sudden reversion to a more babyish state, when thumb goes back into mouth and competence seems to fly out of the window. Alistair, who was four and three-quarters, illustrated this when every afternoon on getting back from school he would go to the family computer and try to do a maths program that was, in fact, much too difficult for him. "Look what I can do!" he exclaimed joyously when he got something right. This was followed by an "I'm bored now," to cover the fact that he couldn't yet do the more tricky sums. Then, sucking hard on his fingers, he would curl up on his mother's lap as if he needed to regain a place where he didn't have to be "clever" or a "big boy". He could just be Mummy's baby until he was ready once again to run off and discover new things.

Children of this age are often so exhausted by a school day, even by a day in nursery, that when they get home they can become quite fractious. Parents can be left bemused by compliments on their child's exemplary behaviour outside the house when at home he is quite the opposite. An exasperated mother trying to cope with tears and tantrums will wonder why her child cannot sometimes behave so well with her. But it is only at home that the child feels safe enough, and loved enough, to let these more negative feelings show. He might have had intolerable feelings of being small and stupid that he has had to hold in check all day. There is also some testing going on of the mother's capacity to tolerate this less likeable side of her child, and also to keep firm boundaries without retaliating. Children are very good at stirring up feelings in the parent that are all too reminiscent of the adult's own four- to five-year-old self. This is because primitive emotions can trigger primitive reactions in all of us, however old we are. For example, after repeated provocation from her four-year-old son, David, Christine was surprised to find herself stamping her foot and yelling at him that she wouldn't do it, she wasn't going to, "No! No! No!" in an exact mirroring of David's earlier behaviour.

It can be very useful to remain in touch with what it was like to be that age as it helps parents to put themselves in their children's shoes. Christine also remembered how much she had loved snuggling on the sofa with her mother, being read to. She repeated this with her son, which was something he enjoyed as much as she had.

Relationship with parents

"Daddy will be very cross"

This is the time when children start moving away from their passionate relationship with their parents to form different but sometimes equally passionate relationships with friends, and even their teacher. One little four-year-old, Ben, came home from school one day and said to his mother, "I wish I could have two mummies – you and Mrs Wright." When asked what it was he liked so much about his teacher, he whispered shyly, "She sometimes lets me sit on her lap when she reads us stories." Ben had been quite anxious about his transition to school, and found it difficult to let his mother go at the school gates. Mrs Wright, a plump motherly woman, was clearly sensitive to Ben's difficulty and gave him what he was missing so much: the feeling of his mother's arms around him.

It is easy to get into a situation where a father becomes the rule maker, allowing the mother to be the gentle, comforting caregiver. Sometimes mothers themselves find it difficult to own the parts of them that might be more strict and firm, preferring to attribute these qualities to the father. Paul, aged four and a half, was bashing one toy car against another. His mother, in the time-honoured way, told him to stop because, "Daddy will be very cross if you bash them." Paul's sister, who was listening to this, suddenly made herself go all floppy and collapsed on the floor. His mother switched her attention to her daughter as she scooped her up in her arms, saying with genuine concern, "Oh, poor thing," and stroking her face gently. Paul started bashing the cars together again, even harder. It was only at this point that his mother was able to take the crossness back into herself and find a firm enough voice to tell Paul to stop, without needing to bring the father in. Paul stopped. His mother obviously felt more comfortable in the traditional role of comforter, as she showed with her daughter, but she then managed to find a firmer voice inside her that was convincing without being punitive. Paul was clearly convinced by her because he stopped.

Mothers of sons often say "He always listens to his father" and "I don't know what it is but when I tell him to do something, he ignores me, but as soon as his dad tells him, he jumps." A father can help his child move away from the original two of the mother–infant relationship towards a different relationship involving three people. When all goes well, the father also gives his son a clear message that he cannot take his place in being Mummy's partner, however much he might fantasize about this, and however much he might try to find ways of coming between his parents. A child needs a father – or a mother acting in a paternal way – to be able to work out where his limits are. This is four-year-old Sammy talking about a cardboard box that he and his father had made into a car a few days earlier:

> Sammy runs over to the car and drags it towards his mother. "Who painted on the wheels, Sammy?" asks his mother. "You did," says Sammy. "No I didn't." "Daddy?" guesses Sammy. "No." "It was ME!" says Sammy, laughing. "It *was* you," says his mother. "And who made the steering wheel?" "Me?" says Sammy hopefully. "No, it was…?" "DADDY!" yells Sammy. And then he says quietly, "Everyone needs a daddy." He adds quickly as he looks at his mother, "And a mummy." His mother gives him a hug.

When Sammy guesses hopefully that it was he who made the steering wheel, he shows a wish to be big and in control, in fact, in charge of steering the car, just as he might imagine that Daddy steers Mummy. However, the hesitation in his voice also shows that he doesn't quite believe that he has this capacity. His joy at remembering that it is his father who does this brings about a feeling of gratitude, and an acknowledgement that he still needs a daddy to help him grow up. Because this was Sammy's own realization of his limitations, he did not feel humiliated by his smallness. This is also an example of two joining up together – Sammy and his father – in this case to create something new, which is a central theme in the four- to five-year-old's world. I will discuss this more fully later.

Amanda found it more difficult than Sammy to acknowledge her small-ness and consequent powerlessness to control her parents. She would try to get between them to stop them kissing or showing any physical affection, sometimes directly by going "Yuk!" and sometimes in a less direct way by putting herself in a dangerous place – she would climb onto the window sill, or the back of the sofa, and look as if she was about to fall – which, of course, made the parents jump up and "rescue" her. Amanda's was an extreme case of jealousy and partly arose because of the birth of a baby brother some months before. To Amanda, Mummy and Daddy kissing meant babies and that was to be avoided at all costs. She was painfully aware both of the mother–father couple, which stirred up her rivalrous feelings towards her mother, and the new baby–mother couple, which took her mother's attention away from her. "What about me?" she seemed to be saying.

There are many children like Amanda who often have the same idea as their brothers that they would make much better partners to the opposite-sex parent than their own parent does. These are, of course, only fantasies, and both boys and girls need firm boundaries to remind them gently of their place as a child. Little girls can become quite seductive when their fathers are around, as four-year-old Emily showed one day when her mother was out and her father was looking after her: "Dad, Dad! Look at me! Look at what I can do! Look, Dad, I'm walking upside down on my hands. And now look! I can do the splits!" Dad responded to this by praising her and then he suggested that she show her mother too when she got back. This reminded Emily that there was a parental couple who could share with each other their delight in their child's achievements, while reassuring Emily that her unconscious fantasy (i.e. something that Emily is not conscious of thinking but which exists in the deeper reaches of her mind) of getting rid of her mother to have her father all to herself would never become a reality.

Some children continue to believe that they have the power to control their parents' actions, although this can simply be a magical wish rather than a firm belief. A five-year-old girl, Olivia, who was an only child, announced while playing with her baby doll that, "My daddy wants my mummy to have another baby but there's no way *that*'s going to happen!" It's hard to know if she really thought she could somehow prevent her parents from creating a rival to her, or if she just couldn't bear the possibility of it. She had had five years of being the only one. There seemed to be, as with Emily, a secret feeling that she would be the better partner for Daddy, and if any babies were going to come along, Daddy should be giving them to her, not to Mummy – after all, look how well she could care for her baby doll!

Five is the age when traditionally children put these passionate feelings about their parents aside, in order to be able to concentrate on the business of learning and acquiring knowledge about their outside world. They won't surface again until puberty, but that's another story.

Sibling rivalry

"He took my sweets! I hate him!"

Siblings can show amazingly aggressive and hostile feelings towards one another, as well as loyalty and friendship. Nobody knows better how to tease until exploding point is reached. Charlotte, nearly six, was playing happily with her brother Toby, aged four, until Toby, with a wicked grin, distracted Charlotte in order to steal the bag of sweets she had wedged by her side. When she noticed, she sprang up from her chair and lunged at the bag but Toby held on tightly and then kicked her hard in the stomach. Charlotte clutched her tummy and yelled for her father. When he came in and ordered Toby to give the sweets back, he did so but only after slowly and deliberately taking one of the sweets and popping it into his mouth, still grinning in a very provocative way. Charlotte yelled again. A little later on, both children went to play in the garden. They got onto the see-saw together and for a time enjoyed seeing who could make the other go higher. But then Toby got bored and tried to get off, which caused Charlotte to lose her balance and fall. "Stupid boy!" she said and hit him on the arm. Toby retaliated by pushing her and then they were locked together, using both arms and legs to try to make the other fall. Toby broke free and turned to pick up a bamboo stick which he then pointed at Charlotte menacingly. "Don't, Toby," screamed Charlotte, and she ran into the house, shouting "Mummy! Mummy!"

In both these episodes brother and sister started playing cooperatively together until one did something that enraged the other. Things escalated to such an extent that it looked at one point as if they might really hurt each other. It was interesting that first their father was summoned to sort things out and in the later incident it was their mother who was needed as protector.

William, who was in reception class, was quite a leader and would boss the other children around relentlessly, except one day when he fell and cut his knee badly. While he was waiting for a bandage, he began to talk about his two-year-old "baby sister", Katy, and how naughty she was. There was a long story about a broken tap in the bathroom which meant that when his mother was giving them a bath, she had to fill a jug to bathe them. Katy would tip all the water over the floor. "And she pulls my hair and she spoils my toys." When asked what William did when this happened, he said simply that he went to his room and stayed there "to get away from her". Perhaps this was why William had to assert his authority over the other children. He clearly felt quite helpless in the face of his sister's "naughtiness". It seemed too that he was able to express his jealousy and anger towards Katy at the point when he was hurt and needed his mother, and Katy was the one who had got her. "It's not fair!" he said. "Why should she be at home with Mummy when she's so naughty? I hate her!" William's face was tear-streaked and as he was talking, every now and then there would be a stifled sob. However, once he had the bandage on and the pain was wearing off, William seemed to forget about his grievances towards Katy and went off to play happily.

Children like William are reminded of their jealousy towards a younger sibling only when they themselves are thrown back to a stage where they feel the need for mothering. Then, their anger at not having a mummy who is exclusively theirs is heightened, but as we saw with William, once he felt ready to be a five-year-old again, his sister was forgotten and he regained a sense of himself that was more focused on wanting to be curious and exploratory. Katy could continue to be the silly baby – he was the older sibling who could do all sorts of things that were not available to her.

Zoë was a different matter and her negative feelings towards her baby sister were all-consuming. She had been jealous of her sister from the moment of her birth, when Zoë was three and a half. She had had all that time alone with her mother – her father had been posted abroad on army service – and the birth of her sister came as a shock that Zoë had not quite come to terms with. However, Zoë found a way of dealing with her feelings that was never open, but instead maintained her idea that she was the good, responsible older sister. She did this by inciting the baby, Rachael, to do naughtier and naughtier things, and then standing back in a superior way while their mother got cross with Rachael. An example of this was when 18-month-old Rachael was in her high chair spooning food into her mouth. When her mother left the room for a moment, Zoë encouraged the baby to tip her food out and throw it onto the floor. Their mother came back to find Rachael chuckling with glee, food all over the floor and walls, and her sister standing there, arms crossed and looking very indignant. "Isn't she naughty, Mum?" said Zoë, while her mother shouted angrily at Rachael. Zoë maintained this position of being the good capable older sister right through her first year of school, and it affected the way she formed friends. She developed a false competence that led, for example, to her tying up all the other children's shoelaces for them because this was something she had learned to do at an early age. Rachael could be the one to be naughty and dirty and messy and always in trouble. Zoë kept herself identified with her mother and, when she started school, with the teacher, who helped all the little ones do things that she had already mastered. Her teacher found her behaviour rather worrying and was relieved whenever she saw a side to Zoë that was less than competent.

As with Zoë, the birth of a sibling can lead to a sharp disillusionment. The child must come to terms with the fact that he is no longer the only one in his mother's life. He has to learn to share this mother with others, rather as he will have to share his teacher at school later on. There is always the doubt in a child's mind that there will be enough space and enough love for two or more. During this important stage in his development, the four- to five-year-old has to accept that his mother doesn't belong exclusively to him but has other relationships which encompass the father, siblings and friends as well. If he feels loved enough, he will begin to recognize the possibility of having relationships of his own outside the family. There will be times, however, especially when he is feeling anxious, that he will want to go back to being the only one again.

Imaginative play

"I'm pretending I'm all alone in the world"

At five years old a child is beginning to give up his open display of feelings towards his parents, which have been expressed so potently by both sexes up till now by the idea that "When I grow up, I'm going to marry Mummy." Now the image of his actual parent will be overlaid with all sorts of different feelings that he has had towards the parent from infancy. This will give him a composite picture of a mother and a father that he will take inside himself. However, the picture can sometimes be very different from the reality, and parents themselves often fail to recognize this view of themselves when it comes out in play. Many parents have watched their child pretending to be a mummy, for example, but acting out a much harsher version of her than the reality has ever been.

The universal popularity of fairy stories is partly because the theme of wicked parents, or parents who fail to protect their children, is so evident in them. Think of the nasty mother/stepmother sending the children away in *Hansel and Gretel*. In the original version she was the actual mother of the children, but perhaps because it was too frightening for parents as well as their children to contemplate such ruthlessness in a real mother, in later versions she became the stepmother. Snow White's father, as well, is not strong enough to save her from her stepmother. These terrifying fictional parents are made safe by being contained in the pages of a book. This allows the child to explore his inner fears of both real and imagined anger and hostility coming from his parents, and his own anger and hostility towards them. Nobody likes to think that they might sometimes have such murderous feelings inside them towards the one they also love so much, and the more these feelings can be acted out in pretend play the more the child feels that they can be contained and made safe.

Lewis, who was four, was at home playing with his train set. He began acting out a story from *Thomas the Tank Engine* with the engines. However, the story quickly became focused on his particular issues around a controlling and withholding father who he imagined was going to punish him severely for being naughty. He pushed one of the engines into a tunnel. Then he went to a cupboard and got out some bricks. He used these to block the tunnel entrance. He said that "Henry" was very naughty so he has to stay there for a very, very long time. "Naughty Henry!" he exclaimed. He finally let Henry out of the tunnel but then made it crash into another engine, so knocking the other off the rails. "Oh no! What will the Fat Controller say? He will be very, very, very cross. He will put Henry back in the tunnel for ever and ever!"

It seemed as if Lewis was trying to work out what would happen to him if he were very naughty, here represented by his deliberately making one thing crash into another to dislodge it. It could be that this revealed Lewis's wish to dislodge his father, and "push him off the rails", in order to be the only one for his mother, but the punishment meted out for this wish is indeed severe. In fact, Lewis was building up a picture of what was good and bad behaviour through his play. How far could he go in his bad behaviour before being stopped by a father, portrayed as the Fat Controller in Lewis's game, who would punish him? But note the over-harsh punishment – banishment for ever and ever – which does not allow Lewis much space to be forgiven or to be able to put things right. Parents can be towering, and sometimes frightening, figures of power and authority for children of this age. Simply thinking something bad about the parent may make the child feel inordinately guilty.

As well as feeling guilty for occasionally having a deep-down wish to get rid of the other parent and so leave the field wide open to them, children also often feel frightened of their parents dying and leaving them alone and abandoned. James was a very anxious five-year-old who worried excessively about his mother's state of health. There was no father around to take on the role of protector. James's play frequently reflected this worry. One day he made a spaceship, using two upturned chairs. He then wriggled himself inside and sat there silently, looking sad. When another child asked him what he was doing, he said, "I'm pretending that I'm all alone in the world and my mummy is dead."

Play and work are intertwined at this age. In both the examples given above we can see how real issues are explored, using the protective safety of pretend and imagination. It was Henry who was naughty and had to be punished, not Lewis. James's feelings are less disguised but still he could express his real fears only when pretending to be in a spaceship, perhaps so that he could "take off" if his feelings became too difficult to manage.

Identity within the family
"I'm different. I'm me!"

Most parents would agree that as soon as their child is born he will have certain characteristics that belong uniquely to him. There is the so-called "easy" placid baby, and at the opposite extreme, the baby who seems to do nothing but cry in the early days. This will have an effect on how parents relate to their child and get to know him. It's obviously more of a struggle if you have a child who seems impossible to pacify, and who makes you feel a failure, than one who responds with pleasure and joy at contact with you. However, as the child grows, his identity will change and develop, as will the parents' relationship towards him, as everyone finds a way to fit together in the changing family constellation. A lot will also depend on the child's position in the family, i.e. whether there are already older siblings, or whether he is the first child with more to follow, or indeed if he is going to be an only child. By the age of four, many children will already have had to adapt to the birth of a new baby, and how they handle this will depend very much on the age gap between the child and the new baby, and the relationship they have had up till that point with their parents. A four-year-old will be better able to cope with a new sibling than a two-year-old because by then he will have developed a clearer sense of his own identity. Even so, he might find it hard being expected to be the "big boy" so that Mummy can give all her attention to the new baby. Instead of being big, he might well regress to being more babyish for a time.

Perhaps being a younger sibling is an easier option in a sense, because then there has not been a need to make this huge adjustment – the older brother or sister has been there from the start. Parents too are not so inexperienced and tend to take child-rearing more in their stride. But being a second child can have its problems because there is always an older one who has got there first, and will always, as it seems to the child, be able to do everything better. The problems of having an older sibling are often outweighed by the benefits of having someone there to help develop language and teach the beginnings of sharing and game playing, and also to gang up with against the parents at times!

Mutual love and affection between siblings goes hand in hand with occasional outbursts of hatred and hostility. But where else are children going to learn to deal with these feelings of rivalry and competitiveness, and pure hatred sometimes, if not in the safe environment of home? These experiences play an important role in giving them a good grounding to cope with the inevitable rivalries that will come later in school.

Children who don't have brothers and sisters of their own have a harder time managing these feelings if they come across the equivalent of siblings in the playground for the first time. They may be quite taken aback by the strength and rawness of the emotions other children show, especially when they see children fighting bitterly one minute and then the next, playing happily as if nothing has happened.

Molly, an only child aged five, painted a picture for her mother "to cheer her up". When asked if her mother was sad, Molly said, "Yes, she's very sad, but if I paint her a picture, she will be happy again." Further conversation revealed that Molly thought her mother was sad because she had to work so hard every day, but that Molly could make her happy when she came home by doing something nice for her that would even, as she said, "make her laugh again". As Molly shows, an only child can often feel overly responsible for the emotional state of the parent. After all, there are no siblings to share the burden.

Sometimes parents may see their child only in one way so that he becomes, for example, the clever one, the naughty one, the quiet one or the drama queen. It can be tough for the child because of the weight of expectations, either negative or positive, on him. It can be self-perpetuating too, as the child comes to believe that there is no room for development of other sides of his character. One mother, long grown up and now with two children of her own, found herself reverting to being "difficult" and "bad" whenever she had contact with her younger sister, who from the age of two had been regarded as the good one in the family. This also happened between five-year-old Dan, and his older brother, Ed. Dan was quite clear that he wanted his brother to be the bad one, and was pleased whenever he caught him doing something "naughty" that made his mother shout at him. He could then feel that he was good and "Mummy will love me more." Dan was too frightened of the part of himself that could behave like Ed, so he gave all the bad feelings to his brother in order not to have to feel them in himself. This way of functioning was not very healthy for either boy, but especially for Dan because the more he denied the angry part of himself, the more difficult it became for him to feel it was safe to be "not good". Happily, splits as extreme as this are unusual, though.

Charlotte and Toby, the sister and brother who fought over a bag of sweets earlier in this chapter, were on the receiving end of a kind of intellectual rather than emotional stereotyping. Their mother was very aware of what she called the "boy–girl difference" when it came to academic ability. Charlotte, she said, was reading at Toby's age. She also thought that Toby's speech was slightly delayed compared to Charlotte's. However, Toby could concentrate for longer and was good at maths. But to their mother's surprise, Toby was the more cuddly and affectionate child, moulding himself into her body when he came for a hug, and Charlotte the more angular and difficult to hug. Their mother accepted this difference between them, regarding it as part of their individuality and separate identity.

I think the mother of four-year-old Lewis, whom we met earlier playing with his trains, sums this up well when she describes a very vivid memory of herself at the age of four in the kitchen. She had been pretending to be a ballet dancer but she tripped. As her mother picked her up and comforted her, she said, "You're just like me, always tripping over things." Lewis's mother remembered thinking, "I'm *not* just like you. I'm different. I'm me!"

Emotional development
"I wanted to do it myself"

Just as an infant needs a mother (or primary carer) to understand his emotional states and help make them tolerable for him, so does the four- to five-year-old. Even though he now has language to express himself, there will be moments when he is overcome with feelings that he cannot manage by himself. However, a parent can't get it right all the time and sometimes things will go wrong, making the child feel that nobody understands him. It is not uncommon to see a four-year-old have a full-blown tantrum, just like the two-year-old he was not that long ago. He will probably feel quite frightened at being so out-of-control.

If your child can let you know how he is feeling at that particular moment and be openly furious with the world, it's because he feels that it's safe to express these difficult things, even if you find his behaviour infuriating. He can hang on to the fact that he is loved enough, and will continue to be loved, in spite of his anger. He will not be able to spoil what is essentially a good relationship.

Jade, aged four, was playing on an indoor slide with her six-year-old sister, when her sister gave her a little push on the back just as she was about to slide down. Jade screamed, reached the ground and then crumpled and continued to scream and sob furiously. Her reaction was quite out of proportion to the mild push she had been given. Her mother came in to find out what had happened and at first Jade's anger with her sister made it impossible for her to speak. After establishing that Jade wasn't physically hurt, her mother worked hard trying to guess what Jade was so upset about, by asking numerous questions like, "Is it because…?" "Were you…?" Eventually Jade was able to regain her speech and said clearly but still with sobs, "I didn't want Leanne to push me. I wanted to do it myself." Leanne then explained that she had wanted her to go faster. Her mother calmly asked Leanne to apologize, which she did. The screams and sobs might have gone on for much longer if Jade had not had the sense of a mother who was basically on her side and who really tried to find out what had gone wrong.

Rage and aggressive outbursts are often the last thing a parent wants at the end of a tiring day. But the alternative to this is when a child either buries those feelings deep inside him so that he doesn't have to feel them any more – and you can see this in children who are over-polite or sugary sweet – or when he gets rid of his frustration and anger by "giving" it to other people. We have seen how Dan couldn't bear the idea of any badness inside him and so attributed all the badness to his older brother. This is a common way that children have of getting rid of unbearable feelings. A child who has been teased and bullied at school may well come home and start teasing and bullying his younger sibling, in order to make his sibling have the same horrible feelings that he had had himself earlier on. Now somebody else can feel the small powerless one; he doesn't have to any more.

Some children who keep all their feelings buried inside them find that these somehow come out through their bodies, in spite of their valiant efforts not to know about them. Dan, who was so intent on keeping himself good and his brother bad, had severe constipation, and throughout the day he would expel a lot of wind, which created a strong smell. Emotionally he was holding himself so tightly together, and offloading other feelings into his brother Ed, that it had an actual effect on his body. He became very distressed by the smell coming from him because it gave him a constant reminder of the unpleasant feelings that he couldn't get rid of. Whenever he did finally manage to go to the toilet, it was extremely painful for him. But it wasn't just the physical pain that Dan found so distressing; despite many reassurances from his parents to the contrary, Dan seemed to think that there was something so destructive inside him that if he let it out, everybody would be able to see for themselves how bad he really was. He believed that his mother would stop loving him if she saw what horrible stuff was really inside him. Dan needed professional help to sort out his very mixed-up feelings.

Dreams and nightmares are another way children have of processing all the hostile feelings which are kept at bay during the day. Alex was a fairly happy-go-lucky boy, seeming to take everything in his stride. He had lots of friends and was managing very well at school. But night-times were a different matter and showed how anxious he might have been earlier, although nobody would have guessed from his cheerful behaviour. He frequently had nightmares about planes crashing, and being chased by angry men. His mother related how it was difficult to convince him, one night when he woke up screaming, that there wasn't a real wolf sitting on the end of his bed, watching him. Perhaps the fact that his mother had gone back to full-time work now he was at school all day had made Alex even more aware of his separation from her. He no longer had a known picture of what his mother might be doing during the day while she waited for him to come home. Having to worry about his mother and her well-being in a place that he couldn't picture must have added considerably to his anxiety. He could also have been showing his anger to his mother for going back to work, something that couldn't be expressed openly towards the mother he loved, during the day, but which burst out at night. It certainly had the effect of bringing his mother to his bedside to comfort and soothe him in the middle of the night.

It may be that your child will suddenly develop an excessive fear about a particular object or animal around now. In a way it's easier to be terrified of something like a spider that can be seen and touched, or rather not touched but avoided, than to have a feeling of anxiety and terror that doesn't have a name. A five-year-old, Charles, developed a fear of spiders quite suddenly. It appeared to come, his parents said, after he had watched a nature programme on television which had shown spiders spinning their webs in close-up. He had seen this film with his grandmother, who he was staying with for the first time. In reality, Charles was extremely anxious about being left by his parents to sleep in a strange bed in a house he didn't know very well, although he didn't show this outwardly. He himself had begged to be allowed to sleep there despite some reluctance on his parents' part. When his parents came to collect Charles the following morning, they noticed that he appeared quieter and more subdued than he normally was. On the way home in the car they asked him if he had enjoyed his stay, but all he could speak about was his grandmother bending over him to give him a kiss goodnight and feeling the "horrid, prickly bristles" on her chin. For Charles the bristly kiss had served to highlight the difference between his grandmother and his mother, who gave him his nightly smooth-skinned kisses. This in turn made Charles yearn for his normal goodnight kiss and emphasized his separation from the one who supplied it. He started imagining that his parents would never return for him or that something terrible would happen to them. These deep anxieties became mixed up with the "horrid, prickly bristles" on his grandmother's chin, which probably had, for Charles, some similarity to the even hairier spiders on television. It was only a few days afterwards, when he happened to see a real spider and started to scream uncontrollably, that his parents saw the extent of his fear, but it took them a little longer to make a link between the two events. It may seem extraordinary that the underlying anxiety that Charles had about losing his parents was displaced in such a dramatic way onto a common object of fear.

We all have ways of protecting ourselves from feeling too much and being overwhelmed, just as Charles was overwhelmed by his worry about being separated from his parents. What the four- to five-year-old needs is a sympathetic ear, someone who can listen to his fears without dismissing them or telling him not to be silly while trying to work out what it is that might be causing the problem. It is the trying to work it out, even if you don't manage to, that is helpful, just as a mother tries to work out why her baby is crying without always being able to know for sure.

2

School and the Wider World

Starting proper school

"I was very sad when Mummy left"

Even when a child has been attending nursery school or going to a playgroup since the age of three, it is still a big step to start proper school. There is a certain amount of loss to come to terms with as well as all the gains stemming from now being regarded as a "big boy/girl". There is loss of babyhood, loss of the special one-to-one relationship with the parent, daily separation from the parent, especially difficult if there is another younger sibling still at home, and loss of omnipotence, by which I mean the child's belief that she can control things magically. It can be hard for the parents too, to let go of their child, especially if she is the baby of the family. It is not that unusual for the mother to be the one weeping at the school gate in the morning as her child turns her back on her to walk resolutely, and cheerfully, into school.

A child must also get used to being one of many, all with equal demands and needs, which means learning to share both the teacher and playthings, and being able to wait her turn. How most children negotiate this stage partly depends on what kind of experience the child has had with her primary carer during the first four years or so. If she feels that her anxieties and worries have been thought about and understood in a benign way, she will have an internal picture of a mother/father who is on the whole good and loving, and who has also given her the basis of a moral code (the super-ego) so that she knows what is right and what wrong, even though she will not always be able to put this knowledge into action. This will help her feel supported and secure when under stress, and also give her the security to experiment and to risk trying new things. And thus, if all goes well, she will relish the changing sense of herself in a wider world, while still needing for some time to come a home to go back to where she doesn't always have to be big and self-controlled.

In a primary school in London, children in reception class were gradually prepared for their coming move to Year 1. Reception class had its own fenced-off playground, shared with the nursery section of the school. During the summer term the children started being taken out into the big playground, at first for a short period and then in the last month before term ended, for the whole of the lunch break.

On the very first day of this transition to the big playground what was noticeable was how little and vulnerable the children suddenly seemed in comparison to the older ones, especially the gigantic 11-year-olds whooping around, shrieking and yelling. The four- to five-year-olds looked lost and bewildered. They had got used to being the big ones in the nursery with all the three-year-olds, and now here they were again as the littlest. They tended to keep together in their class group and many of them huddled by the fence of their old playground waiting for the bell to ring to let them back in to the place that felt secure and familiar. One boy said to another, "Let's make the Quiet Garden home. Come on, it's safe there." They both ran off to an enclosed area next to their little playground.

Any kind of transition is going to stir up feelings from a much earlier period again, even right back to those of being weaned or of feeling abandoned because of the birth of a sibling. Robbie illustrated this when the move into the big playground on that first day reminded him of his scared feelings on his very first day at school nearly nine months before. As he was talking he refused to move from his position by the gate that separated the little playground from the big. He spoke about how scared he was now of being "with the big ones" and how all he wanted was to go back into his old place. Then he remembered his first day at school when he was "only four" and "I wanted Mummy to stay and I was very sad when she left but I managed not to cry." Robbie was feeling particularly in need of a mummy at that point because he had just fallen on the hard asphalt of the playground and grazed his hands. He had been, he said, "Trying to keep up with James but he was running too fast." And this seemed symbolic of his struggle between remaining safe in the nursery, but with no room for development and change, and growing up, with the risk of hurt and of not being able to keep up.

When they were taken back to their own playground that day to finish the lunch break, the little ones seemed to become more daring and boisterous once they had their familiar boundaries back again. They rushed around excitedly, pedalling furiously on the bikes and tricycles, narrowly avoiding each other in the process. The noise level rose considerably. In fact, they were imitating the behaviour of the older ones in the big playground.

As the weeks went by most of the children grew in confidence when they were playing in the big playground, and it became difficult to spot them immediately among the older children. Although they still tended to stay in their year group, there were gradual forays into the parts of the playground previously reserved for the big ones. Children who had older siblings in the school generally had an easier time of it, as did those who were not English by birth and who found an older child from the same country as them. In this particular primary school there were quite a few Korean children and the 10- and 11-year-old Korean girls would seek out the two five-year-olds to stroke their hair and generally pet them as if they were sweet little playthings.

Tag became the main game that they played, and cries of "Chase me" "Catch me" and "Can't catch me" rang out. Several big girls got involved in the chasing and they ganged together to keep the little boys – the little girls were not generally involved in this particular game – inside the enclosed space of the Quiet Garden, which they named "the Dungeon". The girls stood guard by the entrance and pushed back any escaping boy. The rougher the girls were the more the boys seemed to enjoy it. The game went on for most of playtime and several playtimes after that. Each time at the same point, just before the bell rang, the positions reversed and the little boys managed to capture the big girls, although it was clear that the big ones were letting themselves be caught. It may be that at this point the 10- and 11-year-old girls were prepared to let the little boys get a taste of what it might be like to be big and strong and masculine: in other words, to act out the 10-year-old males that they were going to become without the risk of being able to frighten and overpower the girls in reality.

Some of the four- to five-year-olds learned to use the climbing frame, which had rope ladders and a fireman's pole. The development of their physical skills helped them to feel more at ease about being in the big part of the school. They began to speak about what it would be like after the summer holiday when they moved into Year 1. Although there was still some fear about the change, this was tinged with excitement too. It was more difficult to imagine leaving their teacher, though, and Amy said hopefully, "I expect our teacher will be coming with us. She wouldn't leave us, would she?"

Bridging the gap between home and school

"My mummy's going to make special cakes when I get home"

Some children will need a more concrete reminder of their parents when at school, as we saw earlier with Ben, who needed his teacher's lap to help him bridge the gap between home and school. This is where books can be helpful – a favourite book read aloud by Mum or Dad can be taken into school to give the child a feeling of keeping her parents with her. Nick took in a book of his about horrible monsters which his teacher read aloud to the whole class. It was very funny and everybody laughed at the rhymes and general rudeness (of the kind that appeals to this age group) of the language. When the class went off to get changed for games, there was much discussion about who their favourite monster was, with a repetition of some of the words describing them. Nick beamed with pride. He said he didn't mind lending the book to Ben for one day because "Mummy read it to me last night and the night before so I can remember it."

Most reception class teachers are very tolerant of the children's need to bring favourite toys or books from home, or to let them make links between what happens at home and what happens at school. The children in one reception class were given the opportunity to talk about their own experiences when they did afternoon register. After saying "Good afternoon, Mrs Walker," a lot of the children would spontaneously mention an event that was going to happen or had happened at home. These varied from, "James is coming round to play with me today and Mummy's going to make special cakes," to, more unusually, "Last Saturday my dad and me met David Beckham."

Children now have language in which they can summon up the image of the parent; they can hold on to the parent symbolically with words rather than need his or her actual physical presence. It is surprising what bits of information about parents come up during the course of a school day. Typical examples might range from "My granny's coming to pick me up today because Mummy's got to work late" to "My daddy's got dry skin on his face and he has to use a special cream" and "My mummy doesn't like eating snails, she says she's never going to eat them again." And, maybe wishful thinking, but showing her belief that her mother and father wanted to do nice things for her, Sophie said, "I think we're going on holiday to the beach, but Mummy and Daddy haven't told me yet because they want it to be a surprise, I think, for me."

It is not necessarily a bad thing that a child should have to come to terms with the difference between having a parent who has a shared experience with her and a teacher who not only does not know her in the same intimate way but also has twenty plus children to deal with. It means that your child will have to find ways of being more explicit and of sometimes having to cope alone or rely on peers to help explain things. Children will discover that they are in an environment where they will learn things in a different way, and have to acquire different ways of expressing themselves. It is very common for a child to come home from school and respond to her mother's question, "What did you do at school today?" with the simple word, "Nothing". While frustrating for the parent, for the child it might well be that the real response is "Everything, but it's too hard to explain"! There is a children's book (now sadly out of print) called *Little Raccoon and the Outside World* which sensitively, and amusingly, addresses this difference, that is, of the known world of home and mother, and the outside world of unfamiliarity and difference.

Beginnings of friendships

"Can I come too?"

The transition to "real" school is often eased if the child can go with a friend from pre-school. Sometimes this is not possible if children go off to different schools. Then it is a question of making new friends. Some children are much better at this than others; it helps if your child is outgoing or self-confident, although it is shy children who seem to benefit the most from a friendship by using it as a kind of protective shield against the rest of the world. What is interesting is that just like adults, children seem to be drawn to other children who are like them in some way. So timid children will often pair up together, as will children who like breaking the rules and taking risks.

Children in their first year of school begin to care about their friends in a different kind of way. On the whole they really want to resolve quarrels that occur, whereas with their siblings they often don't have this wish or simply don't care very much. They also begin to develop a moral code about how they should behave towards a friend, which differs markedly from how they might behave towards their siblings: "It's fine to take a toy from her, 'cause she's only my sister!" says a five-year-old, who was adamant that he would not take a toy from his friend (see Dunn 2004).

It is surprising at this early age how well a child can understand how their friends are feeling, why they might be upset and what might cheer them up. One drizzly day a little girl, Priya, was standing in the playground, cross because her mother had forgotten to give her a waterproof coat to wear. Priya had been lent somebody else's coat for the lunch hour. Priya remained totally still and sad, as if she had been immobilized by the shame of not having her own coat to wear, and also perhaps by the thought that her mother had "forgotten". Did that mean that her mother had forgotten her, Priya, too? There were also cultural issues here because Priya was Indian and her family had been living in England for only the last year. Perhaps Priya was also overcome by the notion that her mother did not understand the English way of life, symbolized by her forgetting to provide that most English of things, a raincoat. Priya's best friend Jodie worked hard to get her to join in a game that she was playing but Priya wouldn't budge. Jodie first tried telling Priya that she had saved her a place and she was waiting for her. Then she said, "Please come, Priya." When this too was met with stony silence, Jodie sighed and said, "Are you sad?" Priya nodded. "Are you sad because of the coat?" Priya nodded again. One minute later Priya ran off with Jodie and played happily for the rest of the lunch hour. Jodie's real wish to understand what her friend was upset about helped Priya to unfreeze and go off and play in a carefree way.

With friendship all sorts of make-believe games can happen, where children can share in an acting out of their fears, safe in the knowledge that there are two or three of them to make it feel less frightening. They can also share enthusiasms and exciting games, and things that simply make them laugh together. Five-year-old James, who (as we saw in Chapter 1) had been playing a game where his mummy was dead and he was all alone in the world, was joined by his friend Robbie, who came up and asked very sweetly if he could come with him to keep him company. Both boys then moved from the scary thought of being all alone and parentless to being companions in an exciting adventure in outer space.

Children can feel quite bereft if their friend is absent from school, as Molly showed one day when her friend, Adam, was absent. She said she didn't know why he wasn't there. Perhaps he was ill. This was said with sadness. Then she brightened as she said she would paint him a picture of a racing car because he liked racing cars – she didn't but he did. That would make him feel better. He would like her picture, she was sure. It seemed as if Molly was making herself feel better too by feeling that she could do something nice for him, something that would be just for him, and that would bring the memory of him closer to her. This was the same Molly who had earlier wanted to do a picture for her mother to make her feel better.

As she started painting the racing car, Molly added that it made her feel lonely at lunch time when he wasn't there because she liked him. Then she said with a giggle, "I love him and sometimes I chase him round the play-ground, and when I catch him, I kiss him. Sometimes I do but sometimes I don't. But usually he runs faster than me." What seemed to be important to Molly was not so much the game of kiss-chase, as ancient as the hills, but the fact that Adam wasn't there to have this kind of relationship with, that is, a kind of excited chasing that sometimes led to a kiss but sometimes not. Molly was left only with anxious feelings about whether Adam was all right.

Identity outside the family

"Miss, Miss, James didn't put his things away"

To a certain extent a child coming to school will bring with her the identity she has formed within the family. The way she behaves at home and her inter-actions with family members will be similar to the way she is with peers and authority figures, who are treated as if they are siblings and parents. Yet this is not the whole story because school will give her the opportunity to test what she knows about herself against the reality of people who are different from her actual siblings and parents, and who might well react to her in different ways. For example, a child who is used to having all her demands met instantly, perhaps because the parents are afraid of tantrums or can't bear to frustrate her, will get quite a shock when this way of behaving doesn't get the same results at school.

Sometimes a child will become the scapegoat for all the bad feelings the other children have but want to get rid of, a bit like Dan, who we met in Chapter 1, trying to give his brother, Ed, all his bad feelings. Archie, who was just five, seemed to be put in this position. Whenever there was a disturbance in the class all eyes swivelled to him. There quickly became an expectation that he was going to be the culprit, and the sad thing was that Archie soon began playing up to this by indeed being the one to distract another child or to do something annoying just as the teacher was talking. He stopped believing that he was capable of doing anything that was good or that needed concentration. On one occasion, when their class teacher asked anyone who thought they could walk very quietly along the corridor without talking to put up their hands, practically the whole class raised their hands eagerly except for Archie. He seemed to have no belief that he could ever behave in a way that was acceptable. He tried to find a way out of this position by starting to tell tales: "Miss, Miss, James didn't put his things away, like you asked him to," or "Look Miss, look what Sophie did. She tore the page," which actually made him even more unpopular. But the class teacher refused to collude both with the other children when they blamed Archie, and Archie when he told tales. This gave Archie a different experience from what happened at home, where because of a mother who was struggling single-handedly to bring up a large family and work, it was often easier simply to blame him. And as could be seen at school, it frequently *was* Archie who got into trouble.

This is similar to the pigeon-holing that sometimes happens in families, that is, a child who is considered to be difficult or naughty feels she might as well be. It becomes self-fulfilling. And this is where school and the outside world can be so helpful to a child who is seen, and who grows to see herself, in one particular way. With luck, and with sensitive adults, there is a chance for her to get a different reaction to her actions.

Cooperative play
"I'll draw a ghost friend for your ghost"

Around this time children move from playing alongside each other to a form of more cooperative play, where there is the realization that something creative can come from working together. Of course, there will always be some children who want to direct the action and others who are happier being led, and yet others who prefer working by themselves. But on the whole children now become more willing to begin to share ideas and combine them to make something more than would have been possible if they had been working alone.

At playtime in the reception class there was a group of three boys, two of whom were adding touches to a picture that had been started by Farid. Farid by this stage was happy to stand back and let the other two take over. All three boys chatted happily about what they were contributing to Farid's original drawing of an aeroplane flying high in the sky. Robert put thunder and light-ning streaking down from the sky and Theo started drawing long dashes of rain that he said went all the way from the sky to the ground. Farid came back and drew a green ghost in the bottom right-hand corner. Robert then drew a friend for the ghost in a different colour. They debated whether the ghosts would get wet or be struck by lightening. They continued talking excitedly about what they were drawing, getting quite caught up in the drama of the picture. When the time came to take the picture from the easel to put in the take-home place, there was no dispute as to who owned the picture. Farid had started it and so it was Farid's picture to take home and show his mother.

One five-year-old was sliding her feet up and down over the base of a basketball net. She said, "My feet are getting all excited because I'm getting new shoes. Look, they're slipping sliding and they won't stop." Another little girl came up and, without asking any questions, climbed on to the base and made her feet go sliding up and down too. As they both slipped and slid their feet, they started a conversation about shoes, which then led to talk about their families (one of the girls was Japanese and the other Indian) and their countries of origin. All the time their feet kept moving in unison.

Competitiveness
"My rocket's faster than yours"

However much a child might wish to play cooperatively, this can very quickly turn into competitive rivalry, especially, as we have seen before, among siblings, but also with friends. Children of this age can have an anxiety about their identity and where they fit at school. The quickest way a child has of making herself feel better and superior, and of ridding herself of those terrible feelings of worthlessness and littleness is to bring her parents into it. For instance, she might say something about them that shows they are better (or richer or cleverer etc.) than anyone else's family.

This conversation overheard in a primary school between three five-year-old girls shows a fairly benign version of one-upmanship:

Rosie: Two cats come into our front garden and dig up all our plants.

Vicky: Well, cats come into our garden and make the rubbish go all over our garden.

Junko: Well! Foxes come into *our* garden and make the rubbish go all over. And Mummy and Daddy get very cross because they have to clean it all up.

Rosie: A fox came into our *kitchen* and sat down! Mummy threw a plate at him, but it was only a paper plate so it didn't break. And the fox just stayed and stayed there for days!

What started as an interesting exchange of information, with Rosie taking on an adult role (she even gave a grown-up sigh of exasperation), quickly became so exaggerated that it was difficult to tell what was real and what was fantasy. Rosie talked in such a way that it silenced the other two. Neither of them could cap the story of the fox actually coming into the kitchen, and the information about her mother throwing a paper plate gave a touch of reality that made it hard to challenge. This was one-upmanship for Rosie who had been the one to begin the conversation in the first place. In the example given earlier where Farid, Robert and Theo were cooperating in creating a picture that had been started by Farid, this sense of having to go one better was absent.

Sometimes children of this age don't need to bring their parents into the conversation because they are very good at creating "It's better/faster/more powerful than yours" situations all by themselves, again in a competitive, but mostly friendly way. Two boys playing in the playground with stickle bricks were competing in this way with the rockets they had made. Their conversation went something like this:

Tom: My rocket can go 100 billion trillion miles.

Kieran: Well, my rocket can go behind [*sic*] the solar system and then come back.

Tom: My rocket can go behind the solar system *and* cut through metal.

Kieran: *My* rocket can do all that and cut through... what's harder than metal?

This went on for some time, with each boy trying to outdo the other, but the game remained mostly good-natured and at the end they decided to join their rockets up to go "even further than 100 billion trillion miles". These boys were friends and quite similar to each other in temperament. They were obviously enjoying pitting their wits and knowledge about the world against each other's, in a way that was fun for both of them.

Competitiveness among this age group is a part of growing up, and as long as it remains basically friendly, there is nothing wrong with it. But if a child is unsure of her own worth, then competitiveness can take on a nasty edge in an attempt to bolster the ego at the expense of making others feel smaller and less important than her.

3

Social Development

Real and make-believe
"Hello, honey, I'm home"

At this age most children have a clear grasp of what is real and what is make-believe. Four- to five-year-olds in shared pretend play often take on identities and roles that give them a perspective on how adults behave in the wider world. Sometimes they acknowledge that they are pretending by allocating roles, for example by saying, "You be the mummy/princess/doctor and I'll be the daddy/prince/ill person." But sometimes they simply go along with what seems like a pre-decided script with everyone somehow falling in naturally with the acted-out story. It was clear exactly what role Ronnie, a five-year-old boy, was playing and what role he wanted his friend to adopt when he marched into the playhouse, saying, "Hello, honey, I'm home. Where are the kids? I've got some chocolate for them. I stole it from a chocolate factory!" His friend immediately became the wife and picked up a doll. She said with an exaggerated tone, "He's been *so* naughty, he doesn't deserve any chocolate. He's been driving me mad all day!" She gave the doll a hard smack on its bottom.

Just as Ronnie knew he wasn't really a grown-up father or thief but a five-year-old boy, so do most children keep a firm hold on the reality of who they are, and use role-playing to see what it feels like to be somebody else, and to do forbidden deeds, like stealing from a chocolate factory. Children rushing round pretending to be Superman like the feeling that they can be all-powerful and do magical things such as fly, but they soon come down to earth when it's necessary for them to do so.

Even when a child has an imaginary friend who has to be treated by the rest of the family as if she really exists – laying a place at table for her, for example – the child knows deep down that he has invented this friend, however much he might insist to the contrary.

One make-believe game that has remained popular over the generations is that where one child becomes the evil witch who goes around capturing innocent victims. Of course, just as wicked stepmothers make frequent appearances in fairy stories, so do evil witches. The line is unbroken from *Hansel and Gretel* to Roald Dahl's truly frightening *The Witches*, in which, as Dahl says with glee, even your teacher or your mother might be a witch! Watching this being enacted every playtime by a group of reception class children, it was striking to see how easily some children fell into the role of witch/perpetrator and others the victims. Although the children were taking it in turns to be the witch, there was one particular child, Carla, who did not make a convincing victim. However, she clearly relished being fierce and frightening. When playing the witch, her voice assumed a menacing growl and her eyes seemed to flash with anger. The two girls who had just been caught by her looked genuinely scared. They pretended to be tied up in a cage and sat with their hands above their heads and eyes tightly shut, neither moving nor speaking, while Carla, the witch, went running off in search of more victims. However, when an adult asked the two girls what they were doing, they said quite straightforwardly, "We're just pretending we've been caught by the witch." They then closed their eyes again and clamped shut their lips. When it was time for another child to play the witch, Carla was reluctant to give in to the thrill of being caught, and then refused to sit with her eyes closed and her hands above her head. But the interesting thing was that the little girl now being witch soon lost interest in trying to catch and imprison others. Just as Carla had fallen naturally into playing the witch, the other little girl fell equally naturally into playing the victim. In her role as witch she wandered off as if she'd forgotten who she was meant to be. The game came to an end. Even at this early age children seem to feel more comfortable in one role rather than the other, that is, playing either the victim or the perpetrator. It is rarer to see a child easily swapping from one role to the other.

There can be a problem if a child starts trying to live in a make-believe world because the real world feels too threatening and dangerous. While sometimes it is useful to be able to escape to a "not real" world where you can identify completely with other characters (and we all do this when we read fiction and get totally immersed in the story) some children might find it safer to stay in that world, because the reality is, for whatever reason, intolerable. But this is often a temporary phase and brought about by something external that can't be faced at that point, like a bereavement or the birth of a sibling or any number of painful things that to a child seems too much to cope with, and that needs putting on hold for a time.

Development of curiosity

"How do mummies come here?"

Five-year-old Jessica stopped colouring in a Mother's Day card and frowned. After a short silence she said, "I don't understand how a mummy comes here. I know she was a baby and her mummy growed her, but where did my mummy's mummy come from?" There was another short silence and then she said, with a sigh, "It's really hard to think about." Four-year-old Tina, thinking about the same thing, announced that she wasn't going to get a husband to "get a baby"; she was going to grow the seeds in the garden "all by myself". This demonstrates the difference in thinking between a child who is just four, and a five-year-old who seems to be trying to work out the very nature of existence. However, they are connected by one thing, that is, an absence. Both have left out the father's part in the process, Tina more consciously and Jessica by getting muddled about the vital link between mummies and daddies. Accepting the coming together of the mother and father to create a third opens the child's mind to all sorts of other links that can and must be made to enable the creation of something else. At four Tina wasn't quite ready to puzzle things out but Jessica was, even though she found it "really hard to think about".

We saw earlier the pleasure Sammy had from joining up with his father to create a car from a cardboard box. Children have been shown to work harder and achieve more when they work in pairs, and this may be for exactly the same reason, i.e. that everything is predicated on an acceptance of the coming together of the parents in order to create something else.

Once a child of this age has accepted that Mummy and Daddy pair up to make a baby, he can put aside his need to know about this and allow his curiosity about other things full rein. This, of course, is a factor in being able to learn. However, it doesn't mean that children stop being curious about how babies are made. Four- and five-year-olds frequently play at being pregnant, as the following example shows. This is Ellie, who is just four, playing with her six-year-old sister, Anna:

> Ellie says in a whiney voice, pulling on Anna's arm, "Come on, Anna, come and play "the baby needs to go to sleep'." Anna pulls her arm away and says she doesn't want to. Ellie disappears for a minute and then comes back with a baby doll dressed in pink. She giggles excitedly and thrusts the doll at Anna, shouting, "Here, Anna, here's your baby, look, it's coming out of your tummy!" Anna takes the doll and shoves it roughly up her T-shirt. She walks around, pushing her tummy out. Then she abruptly takes the doll out and hands it back to Ellie, saying grandly, "Here, Ellie. I certainly don't want to walk around with your baby up my T-shirt." Ellie takes the baby back and disappears into her den.

Although Anna was initially reluctant to join in, she couldn't resist the chance to play pregnant mummy. Ellie herself was clear that it was Anna who should have the baby, perhaps because she felt deep down there was something forbidden and shameful about the sexual aspect of the game. She certainly got very excited about it. And perhaps Anna too suddenly had a flash that what she was doing was too grown-up, which is why she stopped playing so abruptly.

Around now children suddenly find words like "bum" and "willy" hilariously funny. I have seen two five-year-old boys falling on the floor with hysterical laughter every time one or the other said the word "fart". A pair of five-year-old twins had a song that they had made up which they used to sing while dancing round when they were naked after their evening bath. It went, "We are the dirty boys! We are smelly and dirty, our bellies are smelly, our bottoms are dirty, our willies do weeing, our bottoms do pooing!" etc., laughing all the time. While it might have been annoying to have to listen to time after time, there was an innocence about it that made it quite acceptable. It also shows the growing interest in natural bodily functions that five-year-old children have.

Perhaps this is an indication of how children of this age seem to move right away from any overt sexual content to a more childish glee at finding the so-called rude bits of their bodies so funny. Interest in sexual matters is now on the wane, or lying dormant, to give children a breathing space of a few years in order to be able to concentrate on other things, before puberty arrives at around 11 or 12.

Gender differences

"What are little girls made of?"

Children of this age often seem to adopt rather stereotypical male or female roles outside the home, in a search to find their real identity. Perhaps it is only by taking an extreme position at first that they can be more sure of where they actually belong on the gender continuum. In the first year of school, being the same and fitting in is paramount, and there is a strong pull to conform. It is hard to feel that you're different from everybody else in this area when there might be so many other areas of difference to struggle with, e.g. of race, culture, family make-up etc. One surprise in a reception class was to find that not only did some of the children know the old rhyme "What are little girls/boys made of?" but that they repeatedly chanted it to each other, especially when the girls wanted to annoy the boys. Girls tend to play with girls and boys with boys, and most firm friendships at this age are with a same-sex child. As one five-year-old boy put it, "Girls are ugh!"

Parents who discourage their sons from playing with guns, for example, will often find that the most harmless object can be turned into a "lethal" weapon. A reception class was playing shops with plastic food. At first, both boys and girls were taking turns to be either shopkeeper or customer but then one boy picked up a plastic banana and went running off, pointing it at other boys and making shooting sounds. Soon all the boys were running round the playground each with a banana gun, trying to shoot each other. The girls carried on shopping!

What four- to five-year-old boys and girls choose to draw is also an indication of their need to conform to their gender type. Watching three boys drawing a picture on one side of the easel and three girls drawing their picture on the other illuminated this difference quite powerfully. The boys were drawing a rocket about to take off (these were the same three boys who were earlier drawing an aeroplane).They put in violent streaks of smoke and fire at the bottom, and laughed excitedly as each one used a different colour to add to the conflagration. On the other side the girls had drawn a princess dressed all in pink with hearts decorating her clothes. They were whispering and giggling about which of them was going to be the princess first.

In the reception class playground, which was separated from the main playground, the boys tended to go tearing round on bikes or tricycles, laughing loudly when they just missed crashing into each other, while the girls were more likely to form small groups and chat. This, of course, is a generalized description and there will always be exceptions. But it can be hard to accept how very stereotypically girlish or boyish a child can be in a group when at home she or he might show different qualities altogether.

Parents sometimes get unduly worried about their child's seeming over-identification with his or her own sex, but it is usually a temporary phase that the child needs to grow out of at his or her own pace. The more disparaging or critical parents get of their daughter insisting on only pink clothes and relentlessly drawing princesses, for example, the more likely it is that the child will become even more determined to maintain this position. The time to experiment with being different comes with imaginative play, not in the real world of the classroom and playground. Then children can play at being someone else just to see what it feels like. Amy, one of the girls drawing the princess, particularly liked pretending to be a horse going out of control, or a dog that bit and barked and generally behaved rather badly. Some girls take on a daddy role and march round sternly, looking cross and shouting, in a way that their fathers might find a not very accurate portrayal of how they really are! And boys, too, may take refuge in the playhouse in the classroom, to work out what it feels like to be a mummy, as they play with the baby dolls. This all indicates a desire on the child's part to find out who he is and where he might fit in his social world.

The beginnings of bullying

"She made us sad. She's horrid"

Some children cope with any feelings of helplessness and vulnerability by becoming bossy and controlling. One five-year-old Italian girl, Carla (who we met before being the witch) had arrived in England speaking no English whatsoever. After only one year she was completely bilingual and accent-free, but this was at some cost to her emotional development. She bossed the other children around mercilessly, sometimes actually making them cry. Her eyes would flash angrily if anyone dared to disobey her. In pretend games she would allocate parts to each child, regardless of his or her own wishes. What was surprising was how little the others protested at this behaviour. Carla would say grandly, "No, you can't be the princess. I am the princess. You must be my cat." She would then dictate exactly how the cat must behave. On one occasion Carla took possession of the castle in her usual role as princess, and ordered the other three girls playing with her to be her servants. She was playing a game that involved making a birthday cake for her father, the king. It had to be ready before he arrived home. Interestingly, there was a conspicuous absence of a mother/queen in her game. Carla got so excited pretending to get everything ready in time that she failed to notice two of the girls slipping away, hand-in-hand, from the castle. "We don't want to play that anyway," they explained. "She made us sad. She's horrid, isn't she?" And they went off to play their own pretend game somewhere else.

Carla must have arrived in England feeling completely bewildered, and thrown back to that baby state of inarticulacy, unable to express her simplest needs. What could be more frightening for a four-year-old, recently fluent in her own language, than to lose the ability to communicate? That it was her father's job that had uprooted the whole family probably also contributed to the very mixed feelings that Carla was having to deal with. She was at a stage where she could not allow herself to be angry with her father, "the king", for unsettling her. Her very normal feelings towards her father were complicated by the fact that he had put her in a position of being a helpless baby again. No wonder she had to become the princess daughter again and again, in order to restore some kind of identity for herself. The problem was, though, that she used the power of her newly acquired language to bring this about, but at the expense of making real friends. Carla's inability to allow others an equal role in play prevented her from fully integrating. Her difference in terms of culture and language became more pronounced, but she became unpopular not because of this difference but because of how she tried to deal with it.

There was another game that Carla often played that demonstrated her fear of being the victim. This was the witch game, described earlier, where Carla could not bear to relinquish her role as witch to take turns as one of the victims instead. She had always to be the witch herself. This again led to instances where other children lost interest in playing and left Carla alone. There was little argument or quarrelling when this happened, simply a walking away, which left Carla unable to understand what she had done to bring this isolation about. It repeatedly mirrored her feeling of aloneness and incomprehension when she had first arrived in England.

There is a vicious circle that makes children like Carla continue to act in a bullying way to get rid of their unbearable feelings of vulnerability, dependency and most of all, difference. With Carla, though, it seemed that she was behaving in this way as a direct reaction to an upsetting event in her life, which would settle down with time and luck. However, unless there is a sensitive adult who can understand his motives for behaving as he does while enforcing firm boundaries, the beginnings of bullying by a five-year-old may well become something much more sinister as he grows older. A child who feels powerless in other areas of his life will cling on to, and begin to misuse, the only power that he has, i.e. the power to dominate his peers. Margaret Atwood puts it well when she writes about bullying in her novel *Cat's Eye*: "[Children] are cute and small only to adults. To one another they are not cute. They are life-sized."

Loneliness versus being alone
"Go away and leave me alone!"

Occasionally the four- to five-year-old will have enough of socializing and want to spend some time on his own. This is very different from a child who desperately wants to be with others but can't quite find a way to join in. It can be sad watching this happening when you see repeated attempts made by the child to get others to play with him, only for them to go off and do something else.

Arun was one such child. He had found a good hiding place in the playground behind a bush and wanted other children to come and join him. But although he tried to persuade one child after another, none of them wanted to play with him. Arun gave up and spent the rest of playtime creating an adventure involving pirates and being caught, but all by himself. It was an act of bravado but his underlying feeling of rejection and loneliness was all too obvious. Perhaps it was the fact that Arun was an only child and more used to relating to adults than to children that made other children slightly wary of him. He had a very adult way of talking, which was appealing to adults but disconcerting to his peers. It took Arun some months to find a friend who would willingly stay with him and play the same games. Arun became quite possessive of this friend and would get very angry if he wanted to join another group. Gradually Arun stopped wanting to control everything and he was able to let his friend go off with others and wait for him to come back again. While he waited he played quite happily alone, which was very different from earlier on when he had been so desperate.

Some children are natural loners and need periods by themselves when they are perfectly happy. More than that, being alone can lead to bursts of creativity and imagination. A rather precocious five-year-old, who was an only child and therefore used to entertaining himself, wrote his own puppet plays and then performed them, taking all the parts! As long as a child has friends to rejoin when he is tired of his own company, this is a positive thing. However, with so many computer games and games consoles, and the television, of course, to distract and distance a child both from his imagination and from real human contact, there is another kind of aloneness that does nothing to stimulate creativity. In fact, it deadens it. Even at four or five years old a child might start using a portable games console, for example, to avoid having to engage with the real world. One reception class teacher explained that on Mondays she always made sure that the bikes, tricycles and scooters were put out at playtime because the children tended to come back to school with a lot of pent-up energy. She said that the only reason she could think of to explain this was because she imagined they had been largely inactive over the weekend, sitting playing with their computers and games consoles or watching television.

Part of the problem may be that parents no longer feel it is safe, with some justification, to allow young children to play outside in the street or park with other children. If a parent is required to monitor his or her child at all times, and to be available to take him to friends' houses or to after-school activities, it is clearly easier to have him sitting safely at home at other times, even if this means long periods of inactivity. Parents nowadays are expected to do much more for their children than they were in the past – even a game of football in the park with friends requires an adult to take them there and wait for them – and this is on top of their own busy schedules. It is hardly surprising that exhausted parents sometimes welcome the silence that comes when their child is absorbed in a computer game.

It is easy to spot children who don't really want to play alone but, like Arun above, need to work out ways of engaging with other children that will not drive them away, and those who are quite self-composed and happy when they are by themselves. But it is slightly more worrying to see the number of children who cut themselves off from social interaction and from their imagination by playing with electronic games. This is not to say that these kinds of games are all bad. In moderation, they can help a child with hand/eye coordination, and some are educational and can aid the beginning of reading and counting. But a child who has problems with making friends may well find it less of a challenge to relate to a world of virtual reality. As we saw, Arun kept trying to engage with others and he did eventually find a friend to play with. If he had withdrawn from contact by immersing himself in a computer game, he would have made himself even more isolated.

There are also times when a child who is very cross might yell out, "Leave me alone!" when in fact he wants someone to come to him and make him feel better. Every parent will probably have this experience at some stage, with the addition of "I hate you!" and "I wish you weren't my mummy!" The more this can be tolerated at this age the less it may appear in adolescence!

4

Books and Reading to Your Child

Using books to address common fears

"Read it again"

There are so many good children's books around nowadays that it is sometimes difficult to know which ones to choose. Many parents will read books to their child that they were familiar with when they were young. This in itself can act as a link between parent and child in the present, and the parent as a child in the past. A parent who can be reminded of her own states of mind when little will be more easily able to empathize with her child's current feelings and states.

Four- to five-year-old children love having books read aloud to them. In a reception class even the most disruptive and fidgety children will often manage a period of stillness when a book is being read to the whole group, especially if it has short catchy sentences with lots of repetition. Rhymes and rhythm are important at this stage. In Chapter 2 I gave an example of how helpful books can be in enabling the child to feel a connection between home and school, and mummies and teachers. This was when Nick took in a book of his about horrible – and very rude – monsters. His teacher then read it aloud to the whole class to their great enjoyment, and the book ended up being borrowed overnight by another boy, Ben, so that *his* mother could read it to him.

Books are a good way of taking the anxiety out of a real or imagined situation by making the frightening or disturbing thing happen to fictional characters. By means of the book a child can explore these fears safely and at a distance, but perhaps more importantly, discover that the feelings that she might be experiencing are not unusual and that she is not alone in feeling as she does. In other words, scary feelings can be identified, named and thought about. This may be one of the reasons why a child demands that the same book be read over and over to her, as if by replaying the central theme of the book she can begin to feel some control over whatever her underlying anxiety might be. At this age there is a constant see-sawing between wanting to run back to the safety of her mother's arms, that is, going back to being treated like the helpless and adored infant that she used to be, and the wish to explore her outside world and become independent.

Good books to read to your child

"It's luscious, it's super, It's mushious, it's duper"

One of the best books to help children to come to terms with anxiety is Michael Rosen's *We're Going on a Bear Hunt*. As a family sets off on an adventure that becomes increasingly difficult and more frightening, each page finishes with the words "We're not scared". It is only when the family actually find the bear they had set out to hunt that they can admit to their terror and run back home to safety. The book creates a building-up of tension before an eventual flight away from danger, which is very appealing to four- to five-year-old children, especially as the parents in the story are presented as being as scared as their children while at the same time they continue to protect them from real danger.

The Enormous Crocodile by Roald Dahl contains all the feelings, both good and bad, that children have about themselves. In it, the not-so-good, greedy part that a child might often feel guilty about having is split off into the form of a crocodile. In fact, Dahl has two crocodiles, the crocodile of the title who is swollen with greed and a sense of power, and a "Notsobig One" who can't be tempted by the other crocodile to gang up with him to do "horrid" things. As in all good stories the enormous crocodile is punished at the end, which appeals to a child's sense of right and wrong. It seems just that the crocodile should be so thoroughly punished for his destructive wish to kill little children, and his insatiable greed. This also chimes with many children who have to face the birth of a sibling, with the inevitable mixed feelings that are stirred up; children in this position need to feel that their occasional flashes of hatred for this new arrival cannot do real harm because there are adults around to protect them, just as the other animals in the story make sure that the enormous crocodile does not actually manage to catch and eat a child.

Although the language in *The Enormous Crocodile* might be thought difficult for this age group, children enjoy the sounds of unfamiliar words even
though they might not quite understand the meaning – the story itself is quite
straightforward. When it comes to exposing children to language that might
be considered too advanced you only have to think of Beatrix Potter's book
The Tale of Peter Rabbit, and her use of the word "soporific" to describe the
sleepiness produced by eating too many lettuces. *The Enormous Crocodile* is full
of repetitions of sounds and rhymes which children love repeating. A family
continued to quote from this book when one of the children, now in their late
teens, would ask what was for supper. The reply came:

It's luscious, it's super,
It's mushious, it's duper,
It's better than rotten old fish.
You mash it and munch it,
You chew it and crunch it!
It's lovely to hear it go squish!

It is not surprising that so many books for this age group take up the theme of
being in danger from characters with evil intent, who are bigger and stronger
than they are. Four- to five-year-olds do get scared easily both by the monsters
in their imaginations and by real situations where they are reminded of how
little and how dependent on their parents they still are. You might remember
the reception class children making their first forays into the big playground
and how long it took them to look on the bigger children as mostly benign
and not out to hurt them.

Some children find it hard to acknowledge their continuing dependency
because it raises anxieties about losing the one they still need so much. It is
very common for a child to have a fantasy that she is the orphaned child of a
king and queen, and then for those fantasies to slip over into a real terror of
being left all alone and abandoned by her real parents. How will she survive?
For these children books that explore this kind of fear are particularly helpful.
We've already seen how *Hansel and Gretel* and many other fairy stories deal
with this theme, but a more up-to-date version is the delightful book *The
Gruffalo* by Julia Donaldson, where the main character, a tiny mouse, manages
without help to outwit all the bigger fiercer predators who want to eat him.

The Gruffalo is a book that uses a regular rhythmic pattern which is
unchanging apart from one word, the different animal that the mouse meets

on each page. Just like *We're Going on a Bear Hunt* this makes potentially terrifying situations manageable for the child. It is the familiarity of the sentences which gives the child a sense that she can manage to look at frightening things, and not turn away from them. For example: "A mouse took a stroll through the deep dark wood. A fox saw the mouse and the mouse looked good." Fox then changes to an owl, a snake and finally the fearsome Gruffalo himself. In *We're Going on a Bear Hunt* the same technique is used. Each page on the left has "What a beautiful day! We're not scared." Then on the right-hand page comes the danger: "Uh-uh! A river/Mud/A forest/A cave…" and the realization that the danger has to be confronted: "Oh no!… We've got to go through it!", until the family come to the biggest danger of all: the bear himself. *The Gruffalo* is different because it is the monster of the imagination, who suddenly appears right in front of the little mouse in reality, which has to be faced.

The fear that a child might have of being so wild and out-of-control that she will destroy those she is closest to is expressed most clearly in Maurice Sendak's *Where the Wild Things Are*. The "mischief" is all in Max, a young child, whose "mother called him 'WILD THING!' and Max said 'I'LL EAT YOU UP!' so he was sent to bed without eating anything". Max grapples with his furious feelings by imagining that he is king of the wild things – a false sense of power like that of the Enormous Crocodile. He gives himself the power to tame and control the wild things just as his parents control him by sending him to his room. However, the room also gives Max the physical boundaries he needs in order to be able to calm down. He is physically protected and kept safe, and this enables him to break free from the boundaries of his imagination. It is clearly preferable to wreak havoc in your mind, not in reality.

It does not take Max long to realize that he is lonely and hungry; in other words, when his rage has died away he is able to accept the fact that what he most needs is love and nourishment from "someone who loved him best of all". He gives up his omnipotent belief that he is all-powerful and therefore doesn't need a mummy or daddy when the reality that he is a little boy comes back to him.

The fictional Max is a child like all others, that is, a child who has to find a way of controlling his furious rages and destructive impulses in order to become "civilized". Max is at a more advanced age than an out-of-control two-year-old having a temper tantrum. He is beginning to have a sense of what is acceptable behaviour and to be able to use his thoughts and imagination to bring him back to civilization.

All the stories I have mentioned use children's common fears and their resolution to show how such fears can be made less frightening. That is why they are such useful aids to helping a child to identify with a variety of characters in different situations and at different stages.

There is a benefit for parents, too. Encouraging mothers who have failed to make an attachment to their infants and young children to start reading aloud to them can produce startling results. For a group of mothers who came from very deprived backgrounds and who had not had the experience of being read to, the act of reading a story aloud was a way of communicating with their children, although it sometimes made them very conscious of what they hadn't had themselves. Another mother with an autistic child found that her way in to his world was through books, even though she often had to read the same book to him over and over again. It was the only time that her son would let her get physically close to him.

Reading aloud to your child allows the sharing of a special kind of intimacy and closeness. Most of us can remember being read to either in school or at home. Being sucked into a sometimes scary fictional world while feeling the comforting safety of familiar surroundings is one of the delights of childhood.

5

Anxieties and Worries

Coping with loss

"I hope you don't die"

Every change means leaving something behind in order to experience something new. The four- to five-year-old will already have had to cope with numerous changes, all involving endings and losses of one kind or other, before reaching the point where we meet him now. How a child copes with loss depends very much on the nature of his primary attachments, which is to say that the more secure these are the better he will be able to hold on to the idea that loss and change can also lead to a growth in his development. Perhaps another way of looking at this is to think about why some four- to five-year-old children are keen to try out new things with confidence while others find that any new experience engenders anxiety and panic in them. If a child feels insecure about how loved he is, or if he feels that his parent is emotionally unavailable to him (and there may be many reasons for this such as a preoccupation with a new baby), then change can feel chaotic and terrifying. All the energy that should go on having new experiences may instead be used to hold himself together psychically in order to ward off these horrible feelings of panic.

Carla, the little Italian girl who held herself together by bossing around the other children (see Chapter 3), had lost her country, her culture and her language, as well as her much loved grandparents. But perhaps more significantly for her, she had lost the mother who could be emotionally available to her, because her mother was also struggling with the loss of *her* identity in a country where she couldn't communicate easily. One way of dealing with loss is to deny it, so avoiding such painful feelings. But the problem with this is that a change or a move to something new will then trigger the unresolved feelings about previous losses and leave the child feeling even more precarious than before. "As responses to the risk of loss, anxiety and anger go hand-in-hand" (Bowlby 1988). Carla certainly showed anger in the way her eyes narrowed and flashed as she ordered others around.

Angus, who was four years old, coped with two major changes for him (the birth of a baby brother and his start at full-time school) by exerting control over the video. Every afternoon when he came home from school he rushed into the sitting room and inserted a favourite tape into the machine. He would watch up to a certain point in the story and then rewind the tape to the beginning. He never did allow himself to get to the end but seemed to find comfort in the familiarity of what was known, and required no thought or conflict (or resolution). He knew every word off by heart and would accompany these bits of the film with all the actions as well as the words. He mimicked the video in a way that ensured that there would be no nasty surprises coming. The repetition in every word and action made him feel that he was in control, and when he had had enough of the repetition, he generated his own ending by turning the video off. If Angus had risked using words in a creative way, that is, to have had a dialogue with a real live person such as his mother, he wouldn't have been able to anticipate or control her responses. This would have put him in touch both with his difference and his separateness from her, and also his lack of autonomy over changing events. After watching the same short section ten or fifteen times, Angus curled up on the sofa and went to sleep. This seemed to be his way of regulating and controlling what was acceptable and bearable – clearly, any kind of endings weren't at this stage. It was only when the tape finally broke through overuse that Angus was able to let go of it and move on to another film, which incidentally he was able to watch to the very end without too much anxiety.

Sometimes adults think that at four or five years old a child is too young to be affected by loss or change. It is quite natural for adults to want to protect their child by not telling them the whole truth, but children's fantasies about a painful change or ending are often much worse and more frightening than the reality.

Danny was not told of his parents' separation, only that he and his mother were going to stay with his grandparents, who lived in a different part of the country, for an extended period of time. Danny was excited about this and for the first few weeks enjoyed himself enormously. His grandparents made a huge fuss of him. It was only after quite a long time that he started asking where Daddy was and when he was going to see him again. His mother remained unable to tell him the truth until things came to a head one day. Danny had been enrolled in the local primary school and he was taken along to meet his new teacher and the other children. It was in the middle of term. Danny was not stupid and even he could see that if he was to go to school, this was no longer a holiday. His questions became more insistent until finally his mother broke down and told him that they were going to stay with Granny and Grandpa, and that she and Daddy were not going to live together any more. His mother found it hard to understand Danny's initial reaction to this news until she finally worked out that Danny had thought that his father was dead and his mother had been too upset to tell him — he had noted the whispered conversations between his mother and grandmother which mysteriously stopped when he appeared. His relief was clear when he realized that he would still be able to see his father and, when things had settled down, could actually go and stay with him for weekends and holidays.

The odd thing is that teachers, and other professionals working with children, often have difficulty in telling children when they're going to be leaving. They tend to put off until the latest possible opportunity the announcement that they won't be there next term, giving the children no chance to prepare and get accustomed to their loss. Adults all have their own defences to avoid painful feelings, and it might seem easier in the short term to ignore or dismiss as unimportant any significant changes, or to imagine that slipping away without a proper goodbye will cause less disruption. But the child will be left with the feeling that these things are too terrible to talk about. The dread of something that cannot be given a name will increase a child's anxiety far more than an acknowledgement that something is going to change and can be prepared for.

In a primary school the reception class were made anxious about their class teacher's absence one day. This particular class had a habit of saying during afternoon register, "Good afternoon, Mrs Wright. I love you. I hope you're all right," and other phrases such as "I hope you don't turn into a snake/snail/robot etc." Mrs Wright answered each comment in a good-natured, jokey way. But when she was absent because of illness, the class showed their worry to the supply teacher by saying things like "I hope you don't get ill/die/turn into a skeleton," and such like. When Mrs Wright came back, the class were strangely subdued and most said simply that they loved her and they hoped she was better now. The following week they were back to their normal selves and the comments they shouted out got more and more outlandish, e.g. "I hope you don't turn into a racing car!" Of course, you can't prepare children for unexpected illness but you can be aware of the worry that they might show.

A real bereavement within the family is something that most four- to five-year-olds will not have to face. But it does happen and when it does perhaps that is the time for professional help. It is too much to expect a mother coping with her own grief at the loss of a child or partner, for example, to be able to empathize with her surviving child's distress at the same time. The child himself is likely to have very powerful feelings of guilt, rage and sadness that may need to be heard by somebody outside the immediate family.

If a child can be helped to hold on to a good memory of a lost relationship, and not obliterate it from his mind as if it had never existed, then he can begin to move on to a new relationship with confidence and hope.

Obstacles to learning

"It's really hard to think about"

A child who is too concerned with family problems will not have any room in his mind to take in new things. Difficult feelings get in the way of learning. If a child is filled with anxiety about his very survival or the survival of those closest to him (and I mean this in a psychological way, not in reality) he will concentrate all his efforts on trying to keep himself protected and safe. He will have no space left to be able to allow the kind of mental activity required for learning. In a biological sense the "fight or flight" mechanism will be activated and your child may defend himself against an imagined attack either by attacking in his turn or by withdrawing.

This was illustrated by Errol, a four-year-old boy who had very little speech. He seemed to have an excessive concern for his mother's emotional state. He found it difficult to let her out of his sight partly because he could not imagine that he would be strong enough to survive without her, nor she without him. This was shown by his despair whenever he noticed a tiny bruise or minute cut on his mother's hands or legs, when she returned to collect him, which would cause him to burst out weeping. Any sign of damage was unbearable for him and seemed to confirm his worst fears. But Errol also believed that if he allowed himself to speak, the words that came out of his mouth would be so violent and destructive that they, too, would damage his mother irrevocably. He actually filled his mouth with soggy tissue paper to stop words from escaping, at the same time blocking up a toy crocodile's mouth with paper and then clamping it shut with his hand. When he finally emptied the crocodile's mouth – but not his own – he made the crocodile go round the room biting and ripping everything in its sight.

Errol needed professional help to enable him to separate thoughts and words from actions, and to show him that it was all right to have angry feelings that didn't have to translate into angry actions. Once he had this clear in his mind, he could risk speaking, especially to say that he was "very cross with you. I hate you," without anything disastrous happening as a consequence. He discovered that it was possible, and safe, to hate the one he also loved so much. And once that happened he was ready to turn his mind to other things and begin the process of learning.

Errol is an extreme example of a child who believes that to think something, especially something bad, is to do it. But many four-year-olds may feel frightened of thinking bad thoughts, as if they imagine a grown-up will be able to read their mind and punish them for their badness, or that they will make the bad thing happen in reality. At four there can still be a muddle between what is imagined and what is real, and between cause and effect.

Sarah was convinced that she could magic her baby sister to sleep just by concentrating hard enough. That she usually did this immediately after the baby had been fed and was drowsy anyway did not enter into the equation in her mind. She had got the wrong cause with the right effect! Of course, there was also her underlying hostility towards this baby who was getting Mummy's milk. By "making" her go to sleep, she could get rid of her and have her mother's attention back again. Roald Dahl is very good at tapping in to this belief that young children have. He has created quite a few child heroes and heroines who can change events by using a form of magical thinking. One of these is the girl with the "magic finger" in the book of the same name who simply points towards whatever she wants to change. Then there is the little girl in *Matilda*, who employs her "mental powers" to get rid of her headmistress, among other evil characters.

By the age of five the child's conviction that he can make things happen through magical thoughts has to a large extent died away. This is partly because of the reality testing that happens again and again in the world of school. He will soon discover that he is not in control of certain things and that he can't magic nasty people away however much he might want to!

There are many reasons why a child might not be in a position to learn, and why he may need help with emotional problems before being able to begin the more formal process of learning to read and write, for instance. One striking example of this was Graham, a boy a few months off his sixth birthday, who was unable to make any sense of time. He had been an abused child, removed from his natural mother and placed with a series of foster parents, where he never knew if he was really wanted or how long he was "going to last" there. Graham knew neither how many days of the week there were, nor how old he was. Any mention of time would throw him into a frenzy of violent rage. He could not risk bringing past and present and future together because his short life had been so filled with violence and uncertainty. If he let himself understand time, he would open himself up to facing the pain of a past with a mother who could not protect him when he was a baby and a future with foster carers who were not going to keep him until he grew up.

Over the course of a year, Graham's paternal aunt, who had come forward to care for him, and Graham himself, were helped to build a relationship together of trust. Once Graham really believed that his aunt loved him and wanted to care for him permanently, he began first to notice what day of the week it was and then to talk spontaneously about events that had happened in his past. Finally, he was able to look forward to the immediate future, and then eventually in terms of next year and the year after that. When he had got time sorted out, he was ready to learn to read and write.

This example shows how dramatically emotional factors can get in the way of the learning process, and how equally dramatically there can be a shift in this. Most children are fortunate enough to share a common life with their parents or carers which stretches from past to present and future. The child can relate present experiences to past experiences and so add to his framework of knowledge. And a parent is best placed to understand what her child is trying to say because of this shared knowledge of the child's life up till now. When these things are in place the child can begin to develop intellectually.

Most children will fall between the extremes of Graham and his family situation, and a family life where everything runs smoothly. Children with problems at home can have two ways of dealing with this when they first start school. They can either become disruptive and attention-seeking – for these children even negative attention is better than no attention at all – or they can withdraw and make fewer and fewer demands. However, as we saw earlier with Archie, who became the troublemaker in the class, the role of the teacher can play a significant part in giving the child "the opportunity to experience the hope of other possibilities" (Greenhalgh 1994). It is often the quiet, subdued children who get left out, though, simply because they are not making a fuss. Quite understandably, when a teacher is trying to deal with a class of 25 or more children, it is the rowdy ones who disturb the rest of the class who will tend to get the attention. It takes a sensitive teacher to spot the child who might really be having difficulties when he is not able to verbalize it.

Learning a new skill always involves frustration to some degree. It is how children respond to the frustration of not immediately being able to master something that will have an impact on their future learning. Some will become despairing and want to give up, others try to control the situation by manipulating it, but the lucky ones will be able to retain a curiosity that will enable them to work at a problem with the hope of solving it. The more that children have had the experience of learning from frustration in their past the less they will try to evade the inevitable frustration inherent in new things, or try omnipotently to avoid it.

By learning from frustration I mean for example that a baby who does not immediately get offered the breast when hungry will begin to create an image of the breast that is not there. This is the beginning of thought processes and imagination. An infant who is never frustrated, i.e. who is offered the breast before he even knows that he's hungry, will never have to do this work, and conversely, an infant who is neglected and left hungry will become too anxious to be able to mentalize anything. You can see this in four-year-olds: those who have had too much frustration in the past will give up despairingly when confronted with a new task, and those whose needs have been met too quickly will deal with any new situation with an omnipotence that wipes out waiting and frustration entirely. One boy aged five and a half was a puzzle to his teacher because he was very bright but a long way behind the other children in terms of reading and writing. It turned out that he thought that he didn't have to make an effort but that he would just "know" things in the same way that he believed his father had acquired his knowledge.

Four- to five-year-old children are no different from adults really. We all prefer avoiding a struggle with uncertainty and become angry when frustrated. Everybody longs for simple and immediate answers. But it is the ability to hold on to curiosity that is the key to learning. Jessica puzzling about how she got here, and how her own mummy and granny got here, is an example of this. "It's really hard to think about," she said, but she did go on trying to work it out, unlike Tina, who decided that she could create her own baby without anybody else's help (see Chapter 3).

Illness and other problems

"It's my fault he's ill"

Johnny, who had just turned four and had started in reception class, needed to go into hospital overnight for a circumcision because of a tight foreskin. His mother was sensitive to what this might mean to Johnny, but his older brother, Hugh, wasn't, and raised Johnny's fears considerably by teasing him and telling him that he was going to have his willy cut off. His mother had to give a lot of reassurance to Johnny that this wasn't the case. Johnny's father also added to his fears by expressing aloud his own doubts about having a son who was going to be circumcised not because of his religion but because of medical reasons. What would his son's identity be afterwards? An operation such as this raised fears in the males of the family, which left Johnny's mother as the only one who was able to put a different perspective on things. Older siblings can be particularly cruel in cases like these, perhaps because it stirs up their own doubts about their recently formed identities. Hugh and his father ganged up together at a time when Johnny particularly needed his father to help him feel that something wasn't going to be cut off him to make him less of a man, and therefore different from his father and brother.

Johnny had a play therapist in the hospital who worked with him to explain exactly what would happen in the operation and how he would feel afterwards. Johnny was allowed to "perform" the operation on male dolls and teddies, and all of this put his mind to rest considerably. His brother continued to tease him for some time afterwards but his mother and father refused to take sides and gradually the teasing died down.

When a parent is ill, entirely different feelings are stirred up. A four- to five-year-old child who is grappling with school and the outside world will be unsettled if a parent becomes unable to focus on the changes in his or her child's life because of the parent's own problems. What a child needs, if this happens, is a straightforward account at an appropriate level for him to be able to understand, of what is wrong and what might be put right in the future. I am thinking particularly of a father who suffered a severe clinical depression when his younger son, Rahul, was four and his older son seven. Their mother was naturally preoccupied with her husband's state of health and she withdrew her attention from the children to concentrate on the father. It was thought that the four-year-old would not be aware of his father's changed state. The seven-year-old was told what was going on and therefore had more of an understanding of what was wrong with their father. He was also told that things would get better. Four-year-old Rahul was left in complete confusion. At school he became silent and withdrawn, occasionally bursting into tears at odd moments. It was only when his class teacher requested a meeting with the parents that the matter was brought into the open and his mother realised how frightened her child must have been by the changed behaviour of every member of the family, especially with the withdrawal of interest in Rahul's achievements.

As mentioned before, a child who doesn't understand what's going on but tries to make his own sense of things will usually end up with far worse fantasies and fears than one who gets an explanation, in terms that are suitable for a child, of what is happening. Rahul blamed himself for his father being ill, and thought that his mother had withdrawn her love from him because she was so angry with him for bringing about this state of affairs. Children of this age often blame themselves for misfortunes in the family simply because they feel so guilty for the thoughts they might have had in the past of hatred and anger towards the parent – as we saw earlier, the belief in magical thinking is still prevalent at this age. Part of the parents' job is being able to survive the emotional attacks of rage meted on them by their child. When a parent becomes ill it is perhaps inevitable that the child will think that his mother or father has been unable to survive his rage.

Worrying behaviour
"Will he grow out of it?"
Sometimes your child may start behaving in a way that signals that all is not well in his life. Bed-wetting, loss of appetite, night terrors and constant anxiety could all be clear markers of something going wrong. This may stem from an obvious misfortune such as the ones discussed above, but sometimes there is no definite cause, only that the child is clearly unhappy.

There is growing evidence that children as young as four are showing signs of depression. There has also been a sharp rise in children diagnosed with ADD (Attention Deficit Disorder) or ADHD (Attention Deficit Hyperactive Disorder). More children with communications problems are now being placed on the Autistic Spectrum, with the relatively new term "Semantic Pragmatic Disorder" being used for children who are thought to be at the high-functioning end of the spectrum, but who have difficulties with communication, including learning how to read and write, and with social interaction.

Nobody knows if the increasing numbers of children suffering from mental health problems really reflect more disturbance of this kind or if people are simply more aware of the symptoms and making a diagnosis earlier. It is often the parents who recognize that something is not right with their child very early on and who have to battle with the medical profession to get it recognized and diagnosed so that different options can be considered. It is very frustrating for those parents who, full of anxiety, take their child to be seen by a medical practitioner, only to be dismissed as worrying unnecessarily. Mary was told that her very withdrawn four-year-old son would probably "grow out of it". Yet parents may be right to follow their instincts. There are many adults now who went through their childhoods knowing that they weren't like other children, but who didn't get a diagnosis until well into their twenties. This used to be the case especially for those with Asperger Syndrome, or high-functioning autistic children.

We all now know more about children with Asperger Syndrome thanks to the popular success of books like Mark Haddon's *The Curious Incident of the Dog in the Night-time*. The boy narrator in the book is a good example of an Asperger's child who is "active but odd" (Wing 1996). These children pay no attention to the feelings or needs of the people they talk to, and they have little understanding of how to interact socially with other people. More severely impaired children behave as though other people do not exist. They often avoid eye contact and look through or past you. These children seem cut off and in a world of their own.

All children with autistic disorders have problems with communication but not all children with communication problems are autistic. There could be other underlying reasons, either medical or emotional. I gave the example earlier of a little four-year-old who was afraid of speaking because he thought the words that came out of his mouth might damage his mother.

However, there is no doubt that just as a child finds it hard to bear the uncertainty of not knowing things, so do adults, especially if they are con-vinced that their child has a real problem. A label in the form of a diagnosis can be very reassuring to the parent in these cases. Everything falls into place; all the puzzling behaviour over the last year or two can be given a name. "Now I understand why she's like that," a mother exclaimed with relief. Sometimes, though, a diagnosis can be unwelcome and simply wrong, as Margaret believed. Margaret and her husband had been relocated to the United States with their four young children. She was shocked to hear that her five-year-old son, George, had been tested by the school psychologist, who was advising that he start a course of Ritalin (the drug prescribed to children with ADHD) to calm him down. Margaret had always regarded George as a perfectly healthy, if boisterous, child. It helped that he was her fourth child and third boy. She had had plenty of experience with the older children and had a good idea of what was "normal".

It is often difficult to get the balance right between correctly diagnosing those children who clearly need interventions and children like George, whose "naughtiness" and difficulty in concentrating was temporary and stemmed mostly from the fact that he hadn't wanted to go to the States and leave his extended family and friends behind. He was finding it hard to adapt to all the changes in his life.

A word here about how easy it is to feel guilty: parents are the first to blame themselves for what they think they have or haven't done for their child, and if the child then begins to develop worrying ways of behaving, the guilt is exacerbated. As the well-known saying goes, "A mother's place is in the wrong." A diagnosis can help the parent feel less at fault and more able to focus on the problem. "Useless" guilt can be incapacitating, as opposed to "useful" guilt which helps us to do something differently the next time.

6

Moving On

The need for boundaries

"Oh well, I suppose you can"

All children of this age need parents and teachers who can set firm boundaries without being too punishing. At school your child might well react to having to share the attention of the teacher with all the other "siblings" by trying to push them out of the way, sometimes surreptitiously and sometimes more openly. If a blind eye is turned for whatever reason (and no one is denying that sometimes it's easier to ignore aggressive behaviour and hope it just dies away of its own accord) the child will be left feeling that she's got away with behaving badly, or that the teacher or parent is afraid to set limits, or even that the adult agrees with this way of behaving. This will make her feel even more powerful and tyrannical in a way that will not help her to deal with her destructive tendencies in the future.

Children who have been treated like this will tend to test the limits more and more because in reality they will be frightened of their power to be so tyrannical. "A child who is not given appropriate limits goes in search of them" (Casement 1990), and being able to maintain boundaries in the face of the testing that goes on will show the child that these feelings can be emotionally held and understood. You can often see the relief a child feels when an adult can say a firm "No" to unacceptable behaviour in an emotionally non-threatening way.

This is easier said than done sometimes. As we have seen, some mothers find it particularly difficult to frustrate their child, or they prefer to see themselves as kind and giving, not as rule makers. Jennie, mother of four-year-old Jack, was determined to be different from her own mother, who she felt had been particularly harsh and punitive with her at that age. And she was different until Jack's sister was born and Jack started trying to attack the baby. Her wish to protect the baby conflicted with her wish to be kind and loving towards Jack. She was also taken by surprise by the hatred and anger she was left feeling, which Jack probably sensed and which made him even more frightened. Jennie dealt with all these difficult feelings by trying to deny her own rage and Jack's, but Jack reacted by becoming even more scared and out-of-control. He was left believing that these feelings were indeed unbearable and unmanageable. When a child like Jack experiences a mother who appears to show only love, the child is faced with an illusion that she alone carries all the negative feelings and thus fears that she is not loved or liked at all. One psychoanalytic idea that often takes people by surprise is that of being able to hate. Love from the parents must also include a degree of hate in order for the child to be able to integrate the two realistically. Otherwise, the child will be left only with a sense of hatred which may then become located in the wrong place, as it was located in Jack.

When Jennie gave birth to her second child this made her particularly vulnerable to feelings that she had had herself as the oldest child with younger siblings coming along, feelings that had not really been resolved. How could she function as an adult when there was such a reawakening of her own infant state of jealousy and anger, which she had managed to hide from herself for so long? Jack was lucky; he had a father who could step in and concentrate on him, and also a teacher who was aware of his situation and who was able to tolerate his anger with firmness and understanding.

The mother of Toby and Charlotte – the brother and sister mentioned twice before, first when they were fighting and then in terms of their gender differences – was very good at controlling and stimulating their intellectual development but when it came to physical boundaries she seemed to let them go. They were often in danger of hurting themselves and each other. Karen, their mother, also had difficulties in controlling the amount of television they watched, although she frequently complained that they watched too much. When Toby took charge of the remote control only his father could get it back from him without a full-scale tantrum. Part of Karen's problem was that she wanted to avoid any conflict that might lead to these angry outbursts. This led to considerable confusion about who had control and who could say no to whom.

Toby was a mine of information about subjects which went far beyond what a normal four-year-old would know, but it seemed as if he was using knowing about something to give him the feeling of having some control over his external world. This was not in the sense of understanding it at an emotional level but in order to master his anxiety about not having firm boundaries given to him by a parent. He also wanted to please his mother for whom intellectual achievement was all-important, but perhaps at the expense of providing a different kind of boundary for Toby in which to contain his difficult feelings.

A typical example of this was when one day Toby was in the kitchen looking at a daffodil in a pot on the windowsill. Toby's mother came in and offered him a chocolate biscuit, which he took and crammed quickly into his mouth. He asked for another one. "We don't usually have two, do we?" his mother said. Toby's face went quite red with anger as he began to protest. "Oh well, I suppose you can," his mother said, handing him the plate. He snatched two, to which his mother said nothing. Toby turned his attention back to the daffodil and named all the different parts, one by one. "It has growed and growed," he said. "It was winter and now it's spring. This is called the stem," he said, touching the stalk, "and these are the petals…five petals…one, two, three, four, five…and this is the trumpet." I think this behaviour shows how frightened Toby was of what he saw as his boundless need and greed, which his mother was unable to frustrate or limit. Perhaps his guilt caused him then to show off his intellectual knowledge as a way of appeasing his mother.

At this age a child will have gradual inevitable disappointments – if not with the mother then with other adults – which will allow boundaries slowly to crystallize. Her omnipotent beliefs of before will change into more realistic and achievable ambitions.

Growing independence

Don't one minute say "Be a big girl"
And the next, "You're too little for that"

In order for your child to be ready to loosen the ties of dependency she needs to have had the experience of a mother, or primary caregiver, who has, on the whole, been able to contain her anxiety and give her the experience of being thought about. In other words, a mother or carer who is emotionally attentive and can be curious about her child until the time when she is ready and mature enough to start being curious for herself. It is from this start that she will grad-ually develop the capacity to think and learn, first at home and then at school where a more formal learning process will take place. But, as we have seen, even four- to five-year-olds may regress to behaving like infants again if they are overwhelmed by powerful emotions that they can't make sense of. At these difficult times they will need a mother to take over the thinking for them until they are ready once again to do it for themselves.

Perhaps the most important thing of all for a child of this age is to feel that there is a space for her in her mother's mind where she can feel that she is understood, and where her fears can be named and made manageable. She can then transfer the feeling of having a space in another person's mind to her teachers and friends, and perhaps more importantly, develop a space in her own mind where thinking can take place. Her sense of her identity as separate from but connected to her family will grow stronger, as she sees herself reflected through the eyes not only of her mother but through those of all the other significant people in her life.

Friendships will become more solid and there may well be sleepovers with other children, which can now be coped with without too much anxiety about leaving the parents. Shared fantasies and make-believe play an increasingly important part in a close friendship, leading to a growth of intimacy and of new ways of handling disagreements.

The next few years are called the latency period, and this is roughly from the age of 5 to 11 or 12, the age that corresponds to primary school years. Latency means that the passionate feelings that a child has had until now become dormant until puberty is reached. There is good reason for this period of relative quiet because it means that your child can concentrate all her energy on learning and socializing. Every new accomplishment, ranging from tying her own shoelaces to learning to read, will feel like a huge achievement and add to her growing sense of being able to manage her world.

And so your child will, with luck and love, approach her sixth birthday with the confidence to look outwards. She will turn from the turbulent feelings she had towards her parents, and begin to direct her curiosity towards other kinds of pairings and joining up. The child's wish to know what goes on behind the parents' bedroom door – unguessable things, from which she is entirely excluded – will diminish. With the repression of sexual curiosity she will be able to focus more on all the exciting and interesting things that are happening in her own life. This is the time for learning about the outside world and for learning from her own real experiences.

Conclusion

Urgent Note to My Parents

Don't ask me to do what I can't do
Only ask me to do what I can
Don't ask me to be what I can't be
Only ask me to be what I am

Don't one minute say "Be a big girl"
And the next, "You're too little for that"
PLEASE don't ask me to be where I can't be
PLEASE be happy with right where I'm at.

Hiawyn Oram (1993)

References and Further Reading

Bowlby, J. (1988) *A Secure Base: Clinical Applications of Attachment Theory*. London: Routledge.

Casement, P. (1990) *Further Learning from the Patient:The Analytic Space and Process*. London: Tavistock/Routledge.

Dunn, J. (2004) *Children's Friendships: The Beginnings of Intimacy*. London: Blackwell.

Greenhalgh, G. (1994) *Emotional Growth and Learning*. London: Routledge.

Haddon, M. (2004) *The Curious Incident of the Dog in the Night-time*. London: Vintage.

Oram, H. (1993) "Urgent Note to my Parents." In J. Foster (ed.) *All in the Family*. Oxford: Oxford University Press. Reprinted in S. Gibbs (comp.) (2003) *Poems to Annoy your Parents!* Oxford: Oxford University Press.

Salzberger-Wittenberg, I., Henry, G. and Osborne, E. (1983) *The Emotional Experience of Learning and Teaching*. London: Routledge & Kegan Paul.

Waddell, M. (1998) *Inside Lives: Psychoanalysis and the Development of Personality*. Tavistock Clinic Series. London: Duckworth.

Wing, L. (1996) *The Autistic Spectrum: A Guide for Parents and Professionals*. London: Constable.

Winnicott, D.W. (1964) *The Child, the Family and the Outside World*. London: Penguin.

Books for your four- to five-year-old child

Ahlberg, A. and Amstutz, A. (1991) *Dinosaur Dreams*. London: Heinemann.

Blake, Q. (1980) *Mister Magnolia*. London: Jonathan Cape.

Burningham, J. (1978) *Mr Gumpy's Outing*. London: Penguin (Picture Puffins).

Dahl, R. (1997) "The Enormous Crocodile." In *The Roald Dahl Treasury*. London: Jonathan Cape.

Donaldson, J. and Scheffler, A. (1999) *The Gruffalo*. London: Macmillan.

Donaldson, J. and Scheffler, A. (2000) *Monkey Puzzle*. London: Macmillan.

Donaldson, J. and Scheffler, A. (2002) *The Smartest Giant in Town*. London: Macmillan.

Grey, M. (2005) *Traction Man is Here*. London: Jonathan Cape.

Milne, A.A. (1973) *Winnie-the-Pooh*. London: Methuen.

Rosen, M. and Oxenbury, H. (1989) *We're Going on a Bear Hunt*. London: Walker Books.

Sendak, M. (1967) *Where the Wild Things Are*. London: Bodley Head.

Tomlinson, J. and Howard, P. (2000) *The Owl Who was Afraid of the Dark*. London: Egmont Books.

Waddell, M. and Benson, P. (1992) *Owl Babies*. London: Walker Books.

Waddell, M. and Firth, B. (1988) *Can't You Sleep Little Bear?* London: Walker Books.

Helpful Organizations

Exploring Parenthood
Latimer Education Centre
194 Freston Road
London W10 6TT
Parents' Advice Line: 020 8960 1678
Advice on parenting problems from newborn to adult

Gingerbread Association for One Parent Families
7 Sovereign Close
London E1W 2HW
Tel: 020 7488 9300
Advice Line: 0800 018 4318 (Monday to Friday 10 a.m. to 12 p.m. and 1 p.m. to 3 p.m.)
www.gingerbread.org.uk
Support for single-parent families

Lifeline for Parents
101–103 Oldham Street
Manchester M41 LW
Tel: 0800 716 701 (helpline Monday to Thursday 5 p.m. to 9 p.m.)
Information and support for parents

National Literacy Trust
Swire House
59 Buckingham Gate
London SW1E 6AJ
Tel: 020 7828 2435
www.literacytrust.org.uk
Aiming to improve literacy by promoting the fun of learning and the importance of book choice

Parentline Plus (formerly National Stepfamily Association)
Tel: 020 7284 5500
Helpline: 0808 800 2222 (24 hours a day)
www.parentlineplus.org.uk
Information and support for parents

YoungMinds/National Association for Child and Family Mental Health
102–108 Clerkenwell Road
London EC1M 5SA
Tel: 020 7336 8445
Parents' Information Service: 0800 018 2138
www.youngminds.org.uk
Campaign to improve the mental health of children and young people

Index